A Case Study Approach to Writing Individualized Special Education Documents: From Preschool to Graduation

Kathleen A. Boothe, PhD
Southeastern Oklahoma State University

Andrea R. Hathcote, PhD
Tyler Junior College

Council for
Exceptional
Children

Council for Exceptional Children
3100 Clarendon Blvd, Suite 600
Arlington, VA 22201-5332
www.exceptionalchildren.org

Library of Congress Cataloging-in-Publication data

Boothe, Kathleen A. and Hathcote, Andrea R.

p. cm.
Includes biographical references.

ISBN 978-0-86586-549-5 (soft cover edition)
ISBN 978-0-86586-575-4 (eBook edition)
CEC Product No. P6341 (soft cover edition)

Cover design by Tom Karabatakis, Tompromo Marketing

Layout by Tom Karabatakis, Tompromo Marketing

Printed in the United States of America by Gasch Printing

First edition

10 9 8 7 6 5 4 3 2 1

Dedication

For Patricia...

Contents

Acknowledgements

The authors wish to acknowledge the support of:

Clark for facilitating our face to face meetings, drop-in editing sessions, and keeping us fed and "hydrated."

Andrea's Family for staying out of our way as we worked and for keeping an eye on things while she was away working on the book.

Mickie for asking us if we completed the book so she can use it in her courses.

Marla for texting to ensure we were on task with completing the book.

Kathy's Mom for her encouragement in this venture.

The Council for Exceptional Children Publications Team, especially Al Rickard, for allowing us this opportunity to help the special education community.

We also want to acknowledge our past and current students and colleagues who have taught us so much about quality special education services. You have and continue to inspire us every day.

Kathy would like to thank Andrea for having the "brilliant" idea to write this book. It has truly been a collaborative effort that I would not want to work on with anyone else.

Andrea would like to thank Kathy for being her partner in this project. Writing together has presented some unique challenges, and I am glad we are still friends at the end!

Introduction

A Case Study Approach to Writing Individualized Special Education Documents: From Preschool to Graduation will follow one child, Rochelle, throughout her life in special education. For each primary special education document, you will be given a glimpse into Rochelle's life and needs. Given this information, you can then complete the relevant paperwork.

Case studies are inherently difficult to use to write a good special education document. There are inevitably questions that you will have which will not be directly answered in the case study. Never fear! It is often that way in real life, and we as teachers are called upon to use our best professional judgment and data to provide a solid plan for our students. For this reason, some readers may want to work with others, in a group setting, to discuss all the considerations and obtain other perspectives. Preparing for the Individualized Family Services Plan (IFSP) or Individualized Education Program (IEP) meeting is supposed to be a multi-disciplinary approach, so working in groups is not only helpful, but more realistic. However, you may be the primary person responsible for drafting special education documents in your school. If that is the case, continue through this work alone. You can always ask a colleague for an opinion as you go along.

Children with disabilities often present numerous challenges throughout their educational careers. As they grow and develop and as their lives change, their response to educational stimuli also changes. Special education documents such as IFSPs and IEPs are designed to help service providers clearly describe the services being provided to the child with disabilities. However, these documents are challenging to complete and can be intimidating with all the legal ramifications. We often know what we want to say but writing it clearly on paper while adhering to a technical and lengthy form can be difficult.

Both authors have been teachers who wrote special education documents and professors who have trained pre-service educators to write them. As a result, they know how challenging the process can be. Finding relevant data and information to practice technical writing – as well as developing a quality case study – can be time-consuming, thus we created this case study. We also realize that not all educator preparation programs have embedded field experiences where data can be collected. It is our hope that this book will provide you time to focus on the technical writing aspect of special education paperwork.

About the Authors

Kathleen A. Boothe, PhD, has served the special education community in several capacities. She has been a classroom teacher, a district level behavior specialist, and is currently Program Coordinator and Associate Professor of Special Education at Southeastern Oklahoma State University (SE). Dr. Boothe is currently a member of the Council for Exceptional Children (CEC) and an active member of the CEC Teacher Education Division. She also serves on the board of the Oklahoma Council for Exceptional Children. Her research focuses on improving educator preparation programs, especially as it relates to Universal Design for Learning (UDL) and classroom/behavior management. She presents at CEC Teacher Education Division conferences and has published in several journals such as the *Journal of the American Academy of Special Education Professionals, Preventing School Failure, and Multicultural Learning and Teaching.* She recently won a Faculty Senate Award from SE for Excellence in Scholarship. She loves to travel with her husband and scope out local craft breweries.

Andrea R. Hathcote, PhD, has been part of the special education community as a classroom teacher, administrator, professor, and most importantly, parent of children with special needs. She is currently a professor at Tyler Junior College (TJC) and a member of the Texas Community College Teachers Association. She served as Coordinator of TRIO Student Support Services, a federal grant-funded program providing guidance to first generation students, students from low-income backgrounds, and students with disabilities. In that capacity, Dr. Hathcote was part of the team that wrote a successfully funded competitive Department of Education grant. Her research focus is creating undergraduate research opportunities for freshmen and sophomores within the Presidential Honors Program at TJC. Her work has been published in several journals, including *Preventing School Failure and Multicultural Learning & Teaching.* In 2013, Dr. Hathcote won the Susan Phillips Gorin Award from the Council for Exceptional Children. She is a wife and mother who enjoys traveling the world through the flavors of her kitchen.

CHAPTER 1
Fundamentals of the Book

We created this book to be flexible; it can be used in its entirety, in any order, or on a chapter-by-chapter basis. We did our best to keep the style of the chapters similar, so the reader knows what to expect and how to maneuver through the chapters. For this reason, you will see that each chapter is segmented into the following sections:

- A brief discussion of the relevant content which includes the definition, purpose, and necessary legal components
- Background information and data to write the special education documents
  - Case Study
  - Perspectives from involved stakeholders
  - Assessment results to include data information about academics, behavior, and physical needs, as needed
- A *"Your Task"* section, providing guidance for beginning the writing process

Tips and Ideas for College Instructors and Professional Development Leaders

As mentioned earlier, you may use the contents of this book in any order. Each chapter's case study and stakeholder perspectives will provide the information needed to complete the chapter's specific special education documents. This book was designed to be used as a supplemental text to provide case study data and an overview of the relevant special education paperwork.

We included two symbols to represent areas of discussion. The light bulb will contain "Question(s) to Consider" about the section. We encourage you to use these discussion questions to help your students/trainees think about relevant aspects of the content. From our experience, we understand it is sometimes difficult to think of questions on the fly. The star signifies "Topic(s) for Discussion." These topics are related to special education issues and can be used to connect the case study to your course content. We hope you will find these a beneficial piece of the book.

Resources for more information on the topic are also included in each chapter. These resources have been used in our professional experience and provided to our students or trainees. Finally, the authors did not include any specific document templates because all state documents differ. We highly recommend that you provide your students/trainees with the state approved special education forms.

Tips and Ideas for Self-Study

Professionals seeking to improve their individual skills in writing special education documents can also benefit from this case study approach. Each chapter focuses on a specific special education document, so every chapter may not be relevant to you. Remember that the chapters are divided into sections providing content and a case study. For some, the content may stand alone and can be used to practice writing technical special education documents for their own students. For others, the case study will provide you the opportunity to write these documents without having a personal connection to the student, which may allow you to dig deeper into the actual writing.

Resources are also provided to help you gain a better understanding of the contents of special education documents. Additionally, there are several discussion callout boxes that you may find useful to gain more insight into specific content. Finally, it is very important that you access and use the state and district forms that are relevant to you. Practice with the forms that you plan to use as a professional.

CHAPTER 2
Factors to Consider When Writing Individualized Special Education Documents

Throughout this book, you will gain insight into Rochelle, a product of the foster care system. In chapter 3, you will find Rochelle entered the foster care system under weight and under height, and her speech was unclear. She was not potty trained and had occasional temper tantrums and outbursts. Rochelle had no educational experiences; she had never seen a book or discussed numbers. The first time she rode in a car was when she was removed from her biological parents by the social worker. She lived in a world that was isolated from civilization. As a result, she began her journey intellectually, developmentally, and physically delayed. From this beginning, the case study will take the reader through Rochelle's life through high school. Throughout the chapters you will also be introduced to Rochelle's:

- Brother (Randall): Randall is Rochelle's older brother. He is also under weight and under height, nor can he speak clearly.

- First Foster Placement (Beverly and Art): Beverly and Art have successfully fostered several children over the years. They are well respected by the Department of Family Services, and Beverly occasionally leads a support group for other foster parents.

- Second Foster Placement (Aisha, DeMarcas and Andre): Aisha and DeMarcas are the second foster parents with whom Rochelle will live. Andre is their teenage son. They are religious, community-minded, and very loving. DeMarcas is involved in a mentorship program based at the school. Aisha works full time at the church where DeMarcas is the minister.

- Social Worker (Amanda): Amanda has been a social worker for 17 years with the Department of Protective and Family Services. She says the case of Randall and Rochelle is one of the most severe examples of neglect she has ever seen. She fights to keep Randall and Rochelle as her "kids" throughout their time in foster care. She truly wants them to succeed.

- Boyfriend (Xavier): In middle school, Rochelle begins a relationship with a boy she meets at church. He participates in DeMarcas' mentorship program and comes from a very troubled background.

- K-12 teachers and administrators: A variety of educators will interact with Rochelle, providing wide-ranging levels of experience, philosophies, and reactions for discussion.

- K-12 related service providers: Due to her ongoing needs, Rochelle will receive support from a variety of related service providers throughout her time in school. Like the teachers and administrators, each provides a unique perspective from their experience and philosophy of intervention.

- Others: School Resource officers and physicians will also play a part in shaping the narrative for Rochelle.

The book is written in chronological order, beginning with Rochelle entering the foster care system and Head Start and ends with her preparing for graduation. At each stage of Rochelle's life, we provide information to help you prepare documents related to a student's Individualized Family Service Plan (IFSP) and/or Individualized Education Program (IEP), to include transition plans, behavior plans, and academic goals and objectives.

Although the Individuals with Disabilities Education Improvement Act (IDEIA) provides guidelines for educating students with disabilities, states and districts may interpret those guidelines a bit differently. The forms used to write IFSPs and IEPs differ among states and districts. For this reason, it is recommended the reader follow state and district guidelines. Blank templates for completing these documents are not provided, as it is best for the reader to familiarize themselves with their state's or district's special education forms.

IFSPs and IEPs are blueprints of a special education student's program. Moreover, they are the contract between the school and the family, ensuring that services listed are being delivered. While a child with disabilities is not legally required to make progress, the school is required to document that all services are delivered with high quality, and to report progress regularly to the family. These requirements serve as the accountability measure for the school. As such, their value cannot be overstated. Documents must be well-written, understood by all, and implemented with fidelity.

When writing IFSPs and IEPs, there are several considerations that most textbooks either gloss over, or only mention briefly, but in practice these considerations make a huge difference. It is easy to see which districts and teachers are skilled and experienced writers and which are not.

Stakeholder Input

IFSPs and IEPs are supposed to be the work of a multidisciplinary team. The document presented at a meeting is simply a draft finalized through the course of the meeting. The draft should be clearly marked as such, and suggestions from all stakeholders must be considered. Changes made to the draft during the meeting are common, and the writer should not take offense when a stakeholder makes a suggestion, asks for clarification, or wishes to have part of the document rewritten. As long as the multidisciplinary team agrees to the changes, they can be written into the document. The more input and consideration each multidisciplinary team member provides, the more likely that members will have higher buy-in or investment in the plan developed.

It is always in a teacher's best interest to have all relevant stakeholders supporting the plan. It is highly recommended to send a draft copy home to the families at least five days before the meeting. At the very least, there should be communication by phone or email regarding the proposed goals for the upcoming meeting. This allows time for families to review, interpret, and internalize goals and be better prepared to provide input at the meeting. This recommendation would depend on your district's expectations for communicating with parents and families.

Writing Style

When drafting IFSPs or IEPs, keep in mind that your writing style should be clear, concise and easy to read. Avoid writing in the passive tense. Use specific, clear verbs. Make sure that anyone, anywhere could pick up the document and clearly comprehend the parts you have written. Pay close attention to your specificity in the Present Levels of Academic Achievement and Functional Performance (PLAAFP) and the objectives, whether academic or behavioral. Many special education documents contain language that is vague, and the objectives are poorly constructed. Consider the following statement on a PLAAFP:

Johnny refuses to complete math assignments.

This statement tells the reader very little. What types of math assignments? What does Johnny do instead? This is a better statement:

When presented with a written math assignment, Johnny will wad up his paper, throw it in the trash, cover his head with his hoodie and sleep.

Now, the reader knows exactly what Johnny refuses to complete and how his behavior looks. In the same way, objectives may also be vague and unhelpful. Consider this goal:

Johnny will increase his math output.

It has no observable or measurable components to determine if Johnny has mastered what is expected of him. A teacher would have no clear direction on how to scaffold instruction for mastery. Instead, a more specific goal can provide direction:

Johnny will complete 90% of written math assignments presented to him in class.

This lets the reader know exactly what Johnny is expected to do, when, and how. This goal also clearly indicates when mastery has occurred.

Learning to write technically will become a habit, but in the beginning, pay particular attention to the words you choose. Be very specific and use active voice instead of passive voice. Action verbs and proper nouns will support specificity. Basically, if you can read the goal aloud, and someone else could act it out with no other instructions from you, you have likely written a good goal.

Technicalities of Completing Special Education Documents

Technical writing is a daunting task when you begin. There are legalities which must be observed, and your work will be highly scrutinized by a multidisciplinary team. While it is rare that a draft taken to a meeting is not revised, there are some considerations which may minimize the amount of redrafting to be done.

First, consider that the draft will be written on a district-approved computer system. That system may or may not use standard word processing software, so give yourself some time to familiarize yourself with the software. Use the tutorials the manufacturer provides and learn how to use the software efficiently.

Second, ensure that you have checked all the appropriate boxes. Most software now has a multitude of checkboxes to help maximize efficiency. However, it is easy to overlook a box or two. For example, that omission could mean the difference between the child receiving special transportation or not.

Third, determine how to check your spelling. Many software applications may check spelling and grammar for you as you go, but the words "two," "too," and "to" are all spelled correctly even though they may be grammatically incorrect in a certain usage. Remember to edit your work, particularly for spelling, punctuation, and grammar. While mistakes do happen, it is best to avoid as many of these "typos" as possible.

Common Mistakes to Avoid

Spelling and grammar are at the top of the list, but there are others. If your software application spell checks automatically, be sure to read the proposed change before approving it. Last names have sometimes been "corrected" to highly inappropriate words, and sentence meaning can be lost if the replacement word is not correct. After checking the spelling, be sure to reread your draft to ensure that changes made were actual improvements. Avoid using proper names in a draft, except for the child's name. For example, when the IEP asks who will implement the 15-minute daily pull-out special education service, write "Special Education

Teacher" rather than "Ms. Smith." Ms. Smith may leave, be absent, or unavailable, and if her name is written into the IEP, then she is legally obligated to provide that service, which can spell trouble later. Refer to your district's guidelines on this, as some may require specific names.

Consider whether time increments will need to be written in minutes or class periods. Many times, services provided to elementary school-age children are written in minutes. For example, "Delilah will receive speech/language therapy for 15 minutes, three times per week." However, in some cases, when students attend middle or high school, time increments may change to class periods. For example, "Francisco will receive co-taught math support for one class period per day." While this may not always be the case, noting how your district prefers time to be counted is vital.

Complicated issues may arise in which you will want to seek guidance from your state and district for the most up-to-date requirements. When completing these documents, it is imperative to write *individualized* plans, avoiding copying and pasting from one student's document to another. At their core, these are legal documents which reflect the professionalism of you and your district.

CHAPTER 3
Rochelle Qualifies for Early Intervention Services: Writing an Individualized Family Service Plan

This chapter begins with Rochelle entering a Head Start program and will review the components of the Individualized Family Service Plan (IFSP). At the end of the chapter, you will have an opportunity to practice using the information you have learned to write an IFSP for Rochelle. As you consider IFSPs, keep these questions in mind:

- What is the purpose of an IFSP?
- What is the role of the family in developing an IFSP?
- Who are the members of the multidisciplinary team?

Discussion of Individualized Family Service Plans

Individualized Family Service Plans are required by the Individuals with Education Improvement Act (IDEIA) Part C for babies and toddlers, birth to three years of age, and their families. The IFSP is the first support plan that babies and toddlers with special needs receive when eligible for early intervention services. The major difference between the IFSP and the Individualized Education Program (IEP) is that IFSPs are focused on the family, whereas the IEP is focused on the individual student. Another difference is that the services from the IFSP usually take place in a child's natural setting, most likely the child's home (Stuart, n.d.).

Definition

Under Part C of IDEIA (2004), babies and toddlers are eligible for early intervention services. The specifics regarding these services can be found in the IFSP. IDEIA does not provide a specific definition for IFSPs, but it does note the required components, which we will discuss later in this chapter. According to Bruder (2000), the IFSP is the guide for early intervention services for both the child and their family. The purpose of the IFSP is to plan, implement, and evaluate early intervention services that are specific to the child's and family's needs.

Multidisciplinary Team

The IFSP team is made up of several key members. Stuart (n.d.) recommends the following IFSP members:

- Parents
- Other family members, as requested
- Outside advocate, as requested
- Service coordinator
- Evaluation professionals
- Early intervention service providers (i.e., social worker, therapist, etc.)

Different states may also require additional members not mentioned above. All of these members bring valuable information to the table, but it should be remembered at this level that the focus is on the family, as well as the individual child. Additionally, according to the Early Childhood Technical Assistance Center (n.d.) each state will have their own Part C that complies with Federal guidelines, so it is important to refer to your state's specific guidelines. Because the IFSP is focused on the family, the multidisciplinary team should include people who will assist the parents and other family members, as well as the child.

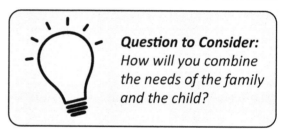

Question to Consider: How will you combine the needs of the family and the child?

Purpose

The purpose of the IFSP is to provide the eligible child and their family with the necessary supports to assist the child in reaching their full potential. IFSPs uniquely consider the family's needs and concerns regarding the child's developmental delays. The IFSP maps the plan to best meet the needs of the child for the stakeholders. An IFSP should be reviewed every six months and must be updated at least once per year (Stuart, n.d.).

Necessary Legal Components

According to IDEIA (2004), there are several parts required in a child's IFSP. Below is a list and brief description of these components.

- Service Coordinator's Information
  - Every IFSP must include the contact information of the service coordinator.

This person is usually the one who works the closest with the child and is most relevant to the child's family.

- **Statement of Child's Functional Ability**
  - o This part of the IFSP will describe, in detail, the child's current abilities and skills. The team will compare the child's current functioning to age-appropriate milestones in the following categories:
    - *Physical*, such as crawling and sitting
    - *Cognitive*, such as thinking and problem solving
    - *Communication*, such as talking and listening
    - *Social/Emotional*, such as playing
    - *Adaptive*, such as self-help skills

- **Statement of Family's Resources, Priorities, and Concerns**
  - o The multidisciplinary team must gather information from the family. This should include the family's resources, such as transportation, strengths and challenges, and proximity to community resources. The family should also discuss specific priorities they have regarding immediate goals for their child and any concerns they may have.

- **Statement of Measurable Outcomes**
  - o According to the Early Childhood Technical Assistance Center (2019), there are two types of outcomes in an IFSP. *Family outcomes* are participation-based or resource-based. *Child outcomes* are participation-based or routine/activities-based.
  - o When writing IFSP outcomes, adhere to the following steps:
    - What is the functional area of need (e.g., playing, sitting)?
    - What routines are affected (e.g., napping, bedtime)?
    - What routines/activities will the child/family participate in (e.g., mealtimes, religious activities, family outings)?
    - What specific behaviors should be addressed (e.g., family conformity at mealtimes)?
  - o Following are examples of specific outcomes:
    - *Child Outcome* - William will play by himself with developmentally appropriate toys using functional fine motor skills.
    - *Family Outcome* - Bob and Betty will attend a community resource fair to locate appropriately trained childcare services.

- **Statement of Transition**
  - The IFSP must include a statement that ensures a smooth transition to preschool services.
  - The following steps may help when planning transition from preschool to Kindergarten (South Dakota Department of Education, 2019).
    - Work with child to gain skills necessary to be successful in school
    - Schedule time to visit future classroom(s) and teacher(s)
    - Observe the child in the preschool setting
    - Invite parents, preschool, and district staff to the meeting
  - A wide variety of transition steps and processes may be observed in states and districts. This is likely because there are no specified federal or legal transition requirements from preschool programming to formal school-age special education services.
  - For more information on transitioning for early childhood, refer to the CONNECT modules created by The Early Childhood Personnel Center and the CEC Division of Early Childhood.
- **Statement of Specific Early Intervention Services**
  - It is important to include where each specific Early Intervention Service (EIS) will take place. It is highly recommended that services be conducted in the child's natural environment, most likely the child's home (Early Childhood Technical Assistance Center, n.d.).
  - If children need services that cannot be provided in their natural environment, such as medical doctors or playgroups, this needs to be mentioned in the IFSP along with information on the funding source and any transportation needs.
  - According to IDEIA (2004), EISs should be evidence-based.
  - When writing EISs into the IFSP, you want to include the duration, location, frequency, length, intensity, and method of service delivery.

Topic(s) for Discussion:
Providing services in a child's natural environment (i.e. home, daycare, or park)

  - **Duration:** When does the team expect the child to have met their goals?
  - **Location:** Where will the EIS take place?
  - **Frequency:** How many sessions will the child receive his/her EIS?

- **Intensity:** Will the EIS take place in a group or individually?
- **Length:** How long will each session last?
- **Method of service delivery:** How will the session be delivered? (i.e. in-person, via Zoom, etc.)

○ If a child is three years or older, then this section of the IFSP should include components to prepare the child for school.

Case Study

As you read the case study, think about the following:

- What are Rochelle's limiting conditions (i.e. cognitive, adaptive, motor, communication, personal/social, ability, and/or achievement)?
- What are Rochelle's behavioral concerns (i.e. emphasis on positive behavior supports and time to adapt)?
- What methods of data collection can be used to evaluate the plan's success?

Rochelle is three years old. She has just begun Head Start at her local, neighborhood elementary school. It is in a rural setting with a high poverty rate. One month earlier, Rochelle and her older brother, Randall, were removed from their home by the Department of Family and Protective Services due to extreme neglect and physical abuse. As a result, Rochelle and Randall are both very underweight and under height. Neither child can speak clearly. They have had no educational experiences. Neither child has ever seen a book, discussed numbers, and the first time they ever rode in a car was when the social worker removed them from their home. They lived in a world that was cut off from civilization and isolated. As a result, Rochelle is intellectually, developmentally, and physically delayed.

While the foster family has worked very hard to help Rochelle potty-train, he still has occasional "accidents." Though unconfirmed, it is suspected that Rochelle has been beaten several times and may have sustained permanent brain damage as a result. Rochelle has occasional temper tantrums and outbursts when denied what she wants. She also tantrums when forced to use words and language to make a request instead of gestures. The

Possible Questions to Consider:
How much of Rochelle's behavior is due to her environment, and how much due to her disabling condition?

tantrums include loud screaming, pulling her hair sometimes to the point of pulling it out, and laying on the floor kicking. She will often tantrum for 5-10 minutes without stopping. Following an outburst, she usually has an "accident" and then sleeps for an hour.

Stakeholder Perspectives

With a new family and the introduction to an educational environment, Rochelle is having trouble adjusting. Her developmental delays are a concern for the employees of Head Start, so an evaluation team is gathering data with the intent to provide support for Rochelle. Each perspective is unique, based on that stakeholder's observations and relationship to Rochelle. As you read through the following concerns, keep their unique perspectives in mind.

Foster Parent Concerns

Rochelle's foster parents, Beverly and Art, are very experienced, having successfully fostered a number of children over the years. They are well respected by the Department of Family Services, and Beverly occasionally leads a support group for other foster parents.

Beverly reports that Rochelle has trouble maintaining routine at home. Rochelle is often impatient for dinner and refuses to sit at the table with the family after she finishes eating. Beverly reports that Rochelle will eat anything put in front of her, but if she does not like it, she will spit the food out wherever she happens to be looking. As a result, Rochelle has spit food on the floor, her plate, family members, and on herself. When directed to clean up her mess, she usually complies, but sometimes she will tantrum. She hates taking a bath and gets out of bed up to five times before finally falling asleep.

Art is definitely Rochelle's preferred adult, and she is more compliant when Art is home. However, Art is a policeman and often works overnight shifts leaving Beverly to care for Rochelle and Randall alone. Rochelle and Randall play well together, though they are often destructive to toys. Rochelle's speech delays are a problem for Beverly and Art. They struggle to understand her but ensure that she at least attempts her speech exercises given by the speech pathologist. Beverly reports that she feels Rochelle is improving, but she still has a long way to go.

Early Childhood Special Education Teacher Concerns, Including Paraprofessionals

Rochelle's teacher, Ina, and paraprofessional, D'Tasha, describe her as a sweet child. They say that Rochelle is desperate for love and will do anything for a hug. She uses mostly gestures to communicate, and the teachers say they cannot understand her language at all. She does tend to eat her meals and snacks very fast and often has trouble napping. During naptime, the teacher has had to place Rochelle's mat away from the other children to keep her from disturbing them. Rochelle has trouble interacting with the other children. She does not seem to understand turn-taking or sharing a space. She will take whatever she wants, often snatching toys right out of the hands of other children. When attempting to use time-out as a punishment, the teachers report that Rochelle will melt down into a tantrum. As a result, they try to redirect her play as much as possible. The teachers report that Rochelle is very sensitive to tone of voice, and if they sound harsh, she will begin to tantrum. Rochelle's foster mother has been called to the school six times in the past month to take Rochelle home because of her tantrums. The teachers are concerned with Rochelle's non-compliant behavior and her sensitivity to being redirected. They also worry about how fast she eats. In addition, her lack of speech is a concern.

Administrator Concerns

Ramona is the current director of the Head Start program Rochelle attends. She has an M.Ed. in Early Childhood Education and a minor in child psychology. She has worked with young children for five years, teaching for three and directing the Head Start program for the past two. Although Ramona is young, she is very knowledgeable about the developmental needs of young children intellectually, emotionally, and physically. She believes strongly in family participation in Head Start and feels that children thrive when surrounded by a positive learning environment that is language rich. Ramona shares Ina's and D'Tasha's concerns regarding Rochelle. Further, she is very concerned about Rochelle's future should she return to her birth parents. Ramona feels very strongly that the Head Start program must help Rochelle gain as many skills as possible in case she is pulled from the program. Although Ramona is passionate about Rochelle's success, she is frustrated with Rochelle's lack of progress. She was hesitant to call Beverly the first time Rochelle was sent home, but no one was able to redirect Rochelle success-fully. Ramona refuses to even discuss any type of punitive discipline beyond time-out and is adamantly opposed to any type of seclusion or restraint. She does, however, recognize the need to put a plan in place to support Rochelle that does not rely on Beverly coming to pick her up.

Family Service Coordinator Concerns

Evan has consulted with the Head Start program for 10 years as its School Psychologist. He conducts all the testing, attends the IFSP meetings, and works with the staff to implement behavior strategies in the classroom. Evan's primary job, however, is at the local university as a professor. He believes strongly in the importance of Head Start, so he works with the local program because they cannot afford a full-time school psychologist. As a result, Evan often sends graduate students and student teachers to the school for internships. While Evan clearly sees and understands the severe neglect Rochelle experienced, he is not overly concerned about her behavior. He has assigned several students to conduct observations of Rochelle in the classroom. They decided the best time to observe was during floor time. Each student is assigned a square, and the teacher conducts a 5-to-10-minute interactive lesson emphasizing an academic skill. During their observations, the teacher was working with the students on words that begin with the letter "m." The graduate students used a frequency recording chart (see Table 3.1) to indicate how many times Rochelle had to be redirected during floor time.

Table 3.1 • Frequency Chart of Redirection Prompts					
	Monday	Tuesday	Wednesday	Thursday	Friday
Number of Redirection Prompts	////	///	//	///	///

The graduate students also conducted classroom observations during center time noting anecdotal information (see Table 3.2).

Evan concludes that the function of Rochelle's behavior is attention exacerbated by her lack of communication skills. Rochelle knows she needs to ask questions or seek assistance, but lacks the socially appropriate means of doing so, primarily language. As a result, she falls back on learned behaviors that elicit the response she desires, namely adult attention. These maladaptive behaviors are so ingrained in Rochelle that Evan advises Ramona, Ina, and D'Tasha that it will simply take time to re-educate her.

Social Worker Concerns

Amanda is the social worker assigned to Rochelle and Randall. She has 17 years of experience working with the Department of Family Services. She stated that this was one of the most severe cases of neglect that she had ever witnessed. When arriving at the home for the first visit, she thought

Question(s) to Consider: *What is the primary concern discussed by each stakeholder? How will this inform your decisions for Rochelle's IFSP?*

Table 3.2 • Classroom Observation Anecdotal Data

	Expected action	Rochelle's actions
Building Center	Use the blocks to create individual or group structures	Banged blocks together to make noise, knocked over other students' structures, had to be removed from center early
Math Center	Use the manipulatives to sort by color, size, and type	Put the manipulatives in her mouth, had to be redirected to spit them out and clean them, moved to next center when prompted
Art Center	Use the crayons to color the provided coloring sheets	Selected a picture of a cat, sat alone and colored, refused to move to the next center when prompted
Book Center	Look at the alphabet, key word, and picture books together or independently	Threw all the books on the floor, redirected to pick them up, once provided a book with cats, sat alone and looked at pictures, moved to next center when prompted
Home Center	Use the toys to simulate home-based activities like cooking and cleaning	Pretended to cook like her "mommy," pretended to feed peers in center, pretended to wash dishes, moved to next center when prompted

the trailer was abandoned. There were piles of trash all around the trailer, and several of the windows were missing. The trailer was in a field off a very long, rutted dirt trail from a county road. When she got out of her car, Rochelle and Randall ran from the door of the trailer to her. They were filthy, wearing mildewed diapers and no other clothing or shoes despite the fact it was November. Their hair was long and shaggy and matted. They were extremely thin. The interview with the

Topic(s) for Discussion:
Importance of obtaining data from multiple sources to make decisions.

birth parents revealed the level of neglect. The birth parents, though dirty, were clothed and overweight. They showed Amanda where they kept the food high on a shelf so "the little 'uns wouldn't get it." The birth mother explained to Amanda she knew how to take care of kids because she had five dogs. Amanda immediately reported the incident, and Rochelle and Randall were removed from the home. The birth parents are required to attend parenting classes and regularly scheduled supervised visits with Rochelle and Randall. Amanda is very concerned about the potential physical problems caused by the lack of nutrition and health care. She was relieved when the children were placed with Beverly and Art because she knew they were in very good hands.

Your Task

You have met Rochelle and her family as well as the members of Rochelle's multidisciplinary team. The team determined Rochelle qualifies for Early Intervention Services.

Your task is as follows:

1. The multidisciplinary team has accepted that Rochelle qualifies for special education and is now prepared to develop an IFSP. Your task is to take on Ina's role as the primary teacher, therefore, the primary author of the IFSP.

2. Determine Rochelle and her family's specific goals and outcomes.

Things to consider:

- Allowing time for Rochelle to assimilate into her new environment
- Funding sources for programming
- Necessity for transportation services to and from outside services

IFSP Resources

Anatomy of an IFSP – www.understood.org (find the search bar and type in "Anatomy of an IFSP")

Early Childhood Transition CONNECT Module – www.connectmodules.dec-sped.org (click "Connect Modules" on menu bar)

IFSP Web – www.ifspweb.org (this site has both blank IFSP forms and a completed example)

PACER Center – www.pacer.org (click on "Learning Center" on the menu bar and then click "Early Childhood")

Wrightslaw – www.wrightslaw.com (find the section on IFSPs, in that section you will find a link to the U.S. Department of Education's Model IFSP example)

Figure 3.1. Individualized Family Service Plan Resources

References

Bruder, M. B. (2000). The Individual Family Service Plan (IFSP). (ERIC Digest #E605). Arlington, VA: Council for Exceptional Children. (ERIC Document Reproduction Service No. ED449634.

Early Childhood Technical Assistance Center (n.d.). Individualized Family Service Plan. Retrieved from www.ectacenter.org/topics/ifsp/ifspprocess.asp

The Early Childhood Technical Assistance Center. (2019). Developing high-quality, functional IFSP outcomes and IEP goals. Retrieved from www.ectacenter.org/~pdfs/knowledgepath/ifspoutcomes-iepgoals/Guidance_for_Trainers.pdf

Individuals with Disabilities Education Improvement Act, 20 U.S.C. § 303.344 (2004).

South Dakota Department of Education (2019). Transition. Retrieved from www.doe.sd.gov

Stuart, A. (n.d.). IFSP: What It Is and How It Works. Retrieved from www.understood.org/en/learning-thinking-differences/treatments-approaches/early-intervention/ifsp-what-it-is-and-how-it-works

CHAPTER 4

Rochelle Goes to Elementary School: Writing an Individualized Education Program

In this chapter, you will learn more about the required components of an Individualized Education Program (IEP) and explore Rochelle's need for an IEP as she transitions to elementary school. After reading the required IEP components, a case study and data will be provided for you to practice, using your state or district form. As you consider IEPs, keep these questions in mind:

- What is the purpose of an IEP?
- What are the criteria for writing quality goals and objectives?
- Who are the members of the multidisciplinary team?

Discussion of Individualized Education Programs

An IEP is a legal requirement under Part B of the Individuals with Disabilities Education Improvement Act (IDEIA) of 2004. The IEP provides schools and families with information on the responsibilities of the school district in providing appropriate Special Education services to eligible students. Each IEP should be based on an individual student, and no two IEPs should look the same.

Definition

IEPs are required by federal law for all students identified with a disability through the IDEIA. Part B defines an IEP as "...a written statement for each child with a disability that is developed, reviewed, and revised in a meeting..." (IDEIA, 2004).

Multidisciplinary Team

IEPs are created by a multidisciplinary team made up of the following required persons:

- Parents
- Local Education Agency Representative (usually the building principal or assistant principal)

- An individual who can interpret data (usually the person who completed the testing)
- General Education Teacher
- Special Education Teacher
- Student (as the team determines necessary)

It is important to note that these individuals need to remain in the meeting for the duration of the IEP meeting. They should not be excused to leave early and able to sign-off on the IEP, even with parent permission, unless they have been through the entire IEP discussion. The IEP facilitator should make arrangements for coverage for anyone who may have to leave, or they should suspend the meeting until all parties can reconvene. The only exception would be for the student. Students should attend their IEP meeting for any length appropriate for their age and ability. For example, a young elementary student may come in, introduce themselves, and tell

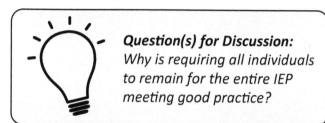

Question(s) for Discussion:
Why is requiring all individuals to remain for the entire IEP meeting good practice?

the team what makes them special or show them a list of their favorite things on a PowerPoint. A middle school student may attend the meeting, introduce themselves, and be an integral part of the discussion over their goals and accommodations.

A multidisciplinary team may also include:

- Related service personnel (e.g. Speech/Language Pathologists, Occupational Therapists, Physical Therapists, School Psychologists, etc.)
- Advocates

These individuals will be invited to attend the IEP meeting if they are a part of the student's program, or as the school or family sees fit. Each related service professional that works with the student should attend the IEP meeting to discuss the student's progress. If a related service professional cannot attend, they need to provide a report containing the student's progress towards meeting the IEP goals and objectives to the IEP facilitator so it can be discussed at the meeting. Good practice would be for the related service professional to call and discuss the student's progress with the family if they cannot be in attendance.

Purpose

An IEP is a legal contract between students, families, and the school. An IEP ensures that all relevant stakeholders are providing adequate services to the student. All services outlined in the IEP are the agreed-upon minimum standards that must be met. Ideally, IEP goals are written in such a way as to help the student with disabilities grow and achieve age-appropriate and grade-level results. However, the IEP should be written with the student's abilities in mind; be ambitious and attainable. The IEP must be reviewed regularly, at least once per year, and progress reports sent to the family. This way everyone remains focused on the student's progress. Ultimately, the IEP ensures that the student's needs are being met.

Necessary Legal Components

IDEIA (2004) requires several components as part of a student's IEP. These components are described below.

- **Present Levels of Academic Achievement and Functional Performance (PLAAFP)**
  - ○ The PLAAFP identifies the student's current functional levels. This should include both strengths and weaknesses. One idea is to "sandwich" the weaknesses in between the strengths. You need to provide data from classroom-based assessments and even high-stakes testing to support your statements. What you put in this section will guide your measurable annual goals.

- **Measurable Annual Goals**
  - ○ Measurable annual goals for special education students must include at least one academic and/or functional goal. These goals depend on the student's needs and are guided by the PLAAFP (see previous section). If it is a weakness in the PLAAFP, it should be a goal in the IEP.
  - ○ Annual goals should be developed collaboratively by the multidisciplinary team and achievable in one academic year.
  - ○ Annual goals must be measurable and specific. Anyone that reads and implements the goal should know exactly what the student will be assessed on. The goal should not leave anything to the imagination. Let's say you want a student, Rashad, to learn to tell time. There are several ways to remember the important pieces of writing goals. One way to remember the parts of a quality goal is that they should be SMART - Specific, Measurable, Attainable, Routines-Based, and Transdisciplinary (Jung, 2007). Another way to remember all the components necessary is LBCC.
    - ▪ **Learner:** The student should be mentioned by name. This is, after all, an *individualized* education program. In our example, this is Rashad.
    - ▪ **Behavior:** The specific and observable task you want the student to perform. For example, if Rashad is non-verbal, perhaps he can move the

clock hands to the correct position. Examples of appropriate terms to make the goal specific and observable can be found in Table 4.1.

Table 4.1 • Terminology for Specific and Observable Goals	
Non-Observable/Measurable Definition	**Observable/Measurable Definition**
Determine	Point to
Describe	Label
Learn	Write
Show	Type
Select	Circle

- **Condition:** The circumstances under which the student will perform the behavior. For example, given a clock manipulative and a verbal prompt, Rashad will position the clock hands at the correct time to the nearest five minutes.

- **Criteria:** The acceptable level of achievement the student must attain. In some cases, this could be a numerical grade, like an 80 on a test. In other cases, it might be successfully completing a number of trials, such as four out of five. Finally, the criteria could be a percentage, such as 70% out of 100%. In our case, given a clock manipulative and a verbal prompt, Rashad will position the clock hands at the correct time four out of five times. So, if you give Rashad five trials to position the hands on the clock, he must complete four of those trials correctly and consistently to meet the goal.

○ Identify how you will measure the child's progress. Examples of measuring a child's progress includes:

- Teacher-made tests
- Observations
- Discrete trial training
- Standardized tests
- Benchmark exams
- Curriculum-based assessments
- Student portfolios

○ Identify how often you will report progress. This should occur at least as often as nondisabled peers. Teachers usually report progress at the end of each grading period by sending a copy of the updated IEP home with the report card.

○ For students taking alternative assessments, benchmarks or short-term objectives must be included.

- **Related Services and Supplementary Aids and Supports**

  ○ Related services are any supportive services, including transportation, that the multidisciplinary team determines will help the student receive a Free and Appropriate Public Education (FAPE).

  ○ These services must be identified in the IEP, as well as (a) if the service will be provided in a group or individually, (b) the projected starting date, (c) the frequency, (d) location, and (e) duration of the service(s).

  ○ Examples of common related service professionals include (remember this list is not exhaustive):

    ▪ Speech-language pathologist

    ▪ Counselor

    ▪ School psychologist

    ▪ Occupational therapist

    ▪ Physical therapist

    ▪ Art/Music therapist

    ▪ Adaptive PE instructor

    ▪ Orientation and Mobility specialist

    ▪ Job coach

    ▪ Social worker

  ○ Special transportation and assistive technology needs must be addressed in the IEP if the multidisciplinary team determines the student needs this.

  ○ Supplementary aids and services are required, which are different from related services. Related services are designed to help students access the curriculum. Supplementary aids and services are designed to facilitate the inclusion of students with disabilities with their non-disabled peers to the maximum extent possible. This action facilitates Least Restrictive Environment (LRE). Supplementary aids and services may include, but are not limited to:

    ▪ Assistive technology

    ▪ Environmental accommodations

- Staff support
- Alternative presentation of content
- Modifications
- Behavioral supports

- **Accommodations**
  - Accommodations are changes made to help students access the curriculum. Accommodations do not change the basic curriculum or reduce the requirements. Accommodations merely change how the student learns the material.
  - The goal of accommodations is to level the playing field, so that special education students can access the same curriculum as their nondisabled peers. *For example*, by wearing contacts or glasses one can complete work successfully. Without them, one cannot clearly see to complete work.
  - Accommodations change the way a student receives the curriculum and/ or how they express their knowledge of the curriculum. *For example*, instead of being responsible for taking their own class notes, the student with disabilities may be provided a copy of a classmate's notes or even an outline provided by the teacher.
  - All teachers are responsible for implementing accommodations. Teachers should be able to document when and how they followed the accommodations. It is difficult to justify how a student failed a course, paper, test, etc. if there is no documentation that shows a teacher attempted the accommodations.
  - Following are accommodations and examples in several key educational areas:
    - **Physical Environment:** preferred seating near the teacher
    - **Instruction:** guided notes to be used during lecture/class presentation
    - **Testing:** separate, quiet location
    - **Grading:** only assessing the items the student completed (i.e., assigned 30 problems, but student only completed 18, so grade would be number correct out of 18)
    - **Homework:** allowing student "study hall" time to complete assignments with teacher rather than at home

- **Modifications**
  - Modifications are changes made to the curriculum in order to meet the student's needs. These are only used when the curricular expectations are

beyond the student's ability level. They will also reduce the requirements of a specific task. Modifications change what the student must learn.

- Modifications to curriculum are created by the special education teacher. These can be changes in instructional level, content, or performance standards.

- Students who receive modifications may not receive a regular diploma, which means they may be unprepared to attend regular college without some type of remedial instruction. Because their curriculum did not follow the standardized curriculum for graduation, many students receiving a certificate of completion will be unable to obtain admission to a 4-year university or college. If they are able to attend a community college, they may need developmental curricula in order to be prepared for college-level content. Therefore, modifying a student's curriculum should only be done when the multidisciplinary team is assured that the student understands the necessity of remedial education or is not capable of attending college after completing high school.

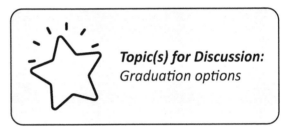

Topic(s) for Discussion:
Graduation options

- **Explanation of Extent/Least Restrictive Environment**
  - In this section of the IEP you will address the amount of time the student will spend with non-disabled peers.

  - You must document when, where, and how long a student with disabilities will be interacting with non-disabled peers. For students in a full inclusion or co-teaching setting, this explanation will be brief. For students with more severe disabilities, the multidisciplinary team may have to be creative and strategic to find ways to provide inclusive experiences. *For example*, students in a more restrictive setting may attend a regular section of music or PE. They also may be included during lunch, recess, or student assemblies as appropriate. In some cases, students may be included during specific classes like English/language arts or math.

- **State Testing Recommendations**
  - You need to address what state testing the student must take and any accommodations he/she will need. Remember, if the student does not use the accommodation on a regular basis and it is not an accommodation in their IEP, it should not be included for testing.

- o Alternative assessments are *usually* reserved for those students who are identified with an intellectual disability and/or receive curricular modifications.

- o If a child needs to take an alternative assessment, then you must include a statement of why they are unable to participate in the regular assessment and why the alternative assessment is more appropriate. You will also need to include the dates, frequency, location, and duration of the student's services and modifications.

- o Remember, alternative assessments are reserved for only the most severely cognitively disabled students in the district's special education population. The actual number of allowances will vary from state to state, but students with mild disabilities will be required to take the on-level assessment that their peers take, perhaps with accommodations.

- **Transition Services**
  - o This needs to be addressed by the time the student turns 16. This can be addressed earlier if

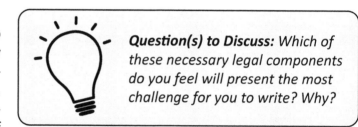

  Question(s) to Discuss: *Which of these necessary legal components do you feel will present the most challenge for you to write? Why?*

  the multidisciplinary team determines it is appropriate.

  - o More information on Transition Services will be addressed in Chapter 6.

Academic Resources

Websites

High Leverage Practices in Special Education –
www.highleveragepractices.org

Intervention Central – www.interventioncentral.org

IRIS Center – www.iris.peabody.vanderbilt.edu/resources

What Works Clearinghouse – www.ies.ed.gov/ncee/wwc

Books

Archer, A. L., & Hughes, C. A. (2011). *Explicit instruction: Effective and efficient teaching.* New York: Guilford Press.

Murawski, W. W., & Scot, K. L. (Eds.). (2017). *What really works with exceptional children.* Thousand Oaks, CA: Corwin.

Figure 4.1. Academic Resources

Case Study

As you read the case study, consider the following key questions:

- What is Rochelle's disabling condition?
- What are Rochelle's most significant academic needs?
- What services can the school provide to support Rochelle's progress?

The caring and committed Head Start team wrote a very supportive Individualized Family Service Plan (IFSP) that allowed Rochelle to make significant progress. Her tantrums decreased from six severe ones per month to less than one per month, and Beverly did not have to pick Rochelle up from Head Start early. Rochelle developed a vocabulary of 190 words, and she weighed 37 pounds and was 35 inches tall when she entered Kindergarten. Although she was still very small compared to her peers, Rochelle ran and played just like they did.

Rochelle and Randall are still in foster care with Beverly and Art, but that will soon change. Beverly and Art only take foster children under school age, and they made an exception in order to keep Randall and Rochelle together. Since Rochelle is turning five and attending Kindergarten this fall, she and Randall will be moved to a new foster home very soon. Amanda will still be their social worker and is working hard to find the right home for Rochelle and Randall. Visits with the birth parents have temporarily ended because the birth parents no longer have transportation and refuse to use the rural bus system. As a result, Rochelle and Randall have not seen their birth parents in more than four months.

Rochelle is attending Extended School Year (ESY) through Head Start this summer, and Beverly and Art arranged swimming lessons. Rochelle is very excited about both. Amanda had planned to transition Rochelle and Randall to their new home at the beginning of August, but two openings became available at the beginning of July. Believing this foster home to be a good fit for Rochelle and Randall, Amanda decided to transition them immediately. This move prevented Rochelle from finishing her swimming lessons.

The new foster parents, Aisha and DeMarcas, are very excited to have Rochelle and Randall. DeMarcas is a pastor at a small, local church, and Aisha is the church secretary and gives piano lessons at the church two afternoons per week. They have one son, Andre, who is 14 and lives in the home with them. Andre is a freshman at the local high school and plays in the high school band. He helps with the children's programming at the church. Aisha was very concerned that Rochelle did not get to finish her swimming lessons and offered to give her piano lessons instead. Rochelle reluctantly accepted the trade, but when she saw the piano and discovered the noises it made, she was thrilled.

In August Rochelle and Randall were enrolled in the local elementary school. The school is much larger than their Head Start school was, more urban, and more multicultural. The enrollment is 780 students. The school serves Kindergarten through Grade 4, and many of the classes are housed in portable buildings spread throughout the campus. Due to high crime in the neighborhood, the campus is heavily fenced. Rochelle and Randall now ride the bus to school each day. They attend the after school program until 5:00 pm, and then the bus drops them off at the church. They wait in the nursery area for Aisha to finish her piano lessons or her secretarial responsibilities. Aisha or DeMarcas check on them frequently while they are playing.

Although Rochelle has a significantly larger vocabulary, she had difficulty with the transition and her behavior regressed. She has been frequently wetting the bed at night and has been found wandering around the house in the middle of the night. Rochelle often refuses to eat, saying that her tummy hurts. When she arrived at Aisha's and DeMarcas's home, Rochelle did not eat anything more than crackers and cheese for three days. Rochelle loves being at the church, attending services, and listening to Aisha's music, so Aisha often plays and sings to Rochelle at home.

With lots of support from Aisha and DeMarcas, Rochelle finally began to make academic progress. She even met standards on her first standardized assessment in third grade. Rochelle is now in fourth grade, and her homeroom class has 22 students. Although Rochelle made adequate progress towards promotion in

Kindergarten through 3rd grade, she is currently showing signs of significant delay in developing her number skills. Rochelle qualified for several Tier 2 level intervention programs, including Reading Recovery and enVisionMATH. Participation in these programs has not improved her progress.

In addition, Rochelle has begun to tantrum more frequently, at least three times per week, usually during math class. Her tantrums include screaming, refusing to comply, pushing furniture (i.e., chairs, desks, shelves) into the walls or other furniture, and pulling out her own hair. In some cases, Rochelle has been so upset that she induced vomiting. Rochelle has been sent to the principal's office

Question(s) for Discussion: *Are Rochelle's significant problems stemming from an academic or behavioral deficit?*

where she cries until Aisha is called to pick her up. With the combination of dramatically slowed academic progress and increased behavior concerns, her teacher has requested that the multidisciplinary team meet immediately to create an IEP and determine which services Rochelle needs.

Stakeholder Perspectives

With the decision to evaluate Rochelle made, all the relevant stakeholders now begin to examine her educational progress. Each perspective is unique and based on their observations and relationship to Rochelle. As you read through these concerns, keep that perspective in mind.

Topic(s) for Discussion: *Stage a mock IEP meeting where participants assume the role of each stakeholder.*

Foster Parent Concerns

Aisha and DeMarcas are very invested in helping Rochelle and Randall. While Randall is responding well and developed a friendship with Andre, Rochelle has been more hesitant to build a relationship. Aisha told the principal that she cannot come to the school three days a week to pick up Rochelle. Her job at the church is considered full-time, and she cannot leave work that often. DeMarcas tried to help with Rochelle, but she refuses to talk to him when she is upset. She only wants Aisha. As a result, DeMarcas has spent more time with Andre and Randall, leaving the bulk of Rochelle's care to Aisha. Rochelle does not tantrum much at home, but Aisha reports being very tired at the end of the day because Rochelle is so needy. Although she is finally eating some, Rochelle has lost weight again, and Aisha is concerned that the social worker will think she is mistreating Rochelle.

General Education Teacher Concerns

Mirah is a first-year teacher. Although she prefers Kindergarten, the only job offer she received was this fourth grade math and science position. Mirah's class is large and her students are very diverse. As a result, Mirah is a bit overwhelmed by her first teaching assignment. Mirah took the time to read Rochelle's file, and she feels very sorry for all the girl has suffered. Mirah decided Rochelle needed extra care and a very loving, tender style of management, but she is completely frustrated with Rochelle's tantrums. Rochelle disrupts the entire class, and it takes Mirah up to 30 minutes to get the class redirected after one of Rochelle's tantrums. Mirah has also received phone calls and visits from several parents of other students in her class regarding Rochelle. Some of the parents expressed concern, some outrage, that their children always report on whether Rochelle had a good day or not. As one parent put it: "Seems like the whole school day revolves around this Rochelle girl. Thought I sent my kid here to learn something." Mirah has filled out the forms to request evaluation for Rochelle, but the principal told her to give Rochelle time to adjust. Mirah then decided the best course of action was to send Rochelle to the principal's office with a referral every time she acted out. As a result, by October, Rochelle has 13 Office Discipline Referrals (ODRs).

In addition to the behavioral concerns, Mirah is very worried over Rochelle's lack of academic skills. Her assessment results demonstrate that Rochelle is well behind in understanding the alphabetic principle, English fluency, and number recognition. The only subjects in which Rochelle exhibits any type of interest or skill is in music, art, and physical education. Mirah reached out to the special education teacher, but since Rochelle does not yet have an official Individualized Education Program (IEP), the special education teacher is reluctant to get involved.

Special Education Teacher Concerns

Leah has been one of two special education teachers at this elementary school for the past seven years. Leah holds a M.Ed. in special education with an emphasis in reading. She is genuinely concerned for Rochelle, not only due to her poor academic skills but being in Mirah's class. Leah thinks Mirah lacks classroom management skills and thinks Rochelle is suffering as a result. Leah is confident that she can improve Rochelle's reading and math skills, and possibly help with her behavioral skills as well, if she is permitted to pull Rochelle from her class for small-group or individual instruction.

Administrator Concerns

Jaime has been the assistant principal of this elementary school for two years. Before that, he was a fifth-grade teacher in a neighboring community elementary school. This is his first job as an administrator. Jaime is very concerned over the number of ODR's Rochelle has received and Mirah's obvious level of stress. He is even more concerned, however, with the parents of other students in Mirah's class who have come to see him. It is obvious to Jaime that Rochelle is a problem child in need of intervention. He is aware of Rochelle's background based on what Mirah has shared with him, and he knows Aisha and DeMarcas from their involvement in the community. While he normally likes to wait until after Christmas to make Special Education referrals, Jaime has decided to push through a referral in order to secure Special Education services for Rochelle. The multidisciplinary team will be assembled.

Topic(s) for Discussion:
Identification through RtI vs. Discrepancy Model

Social Worker Concerns

Amanda called Aisha at the church to check on Rochelle and Randall. She was shocked to hear how Rochelle had been doing in school but was relieved that the school had asked Aisha to sign the permission form for special education testing. She knew from experience that her clients made more improvement when they got extra help in school. Amanda told Aisha to let the school help and to let her know if the kids needed anything. She also told Aisha that the birth parents were requesting visitation again, and that she would be in touch soon to schedule those visits.

School Psychologist Concerns

Delores, a 22-year veteran of the school system, was a bit shocked when she received the paperwork signed by Jaime requesting testing for a fourth-grade student in October. Delores immediately pulled Rochelle's file and read her history. While a pattern of concerns did exist, it was obvious that, at one time, Rochelle was making progress. But a quick perusal of the referral sent from the elementary school indicates that is no longer the case. Delores added the referral to her growing list. She is the only educational diagnostician for the elementary schools. There are two in this district, each with about 700 students enrolled. Right now, their special education population was running about 20% of the total number of students. This was far too high in Delores' opinion. She conducted most of the admission IEP meetings in the district, but the data was there to support the decision. Yes, the schools were urban with poor, mostly minority students, but if a disabling condition is present and the need is documented, the student qualifies. It looked as though she was about to add another student to her growing list.

Delores looked at her packed schedule and cleared time in late October to test Rochelle. Delores called the school to schedule the testing date and location with Leah. She also asked Leah for her opinion. Delores has worked with Leah for years, and they have developed trust. Leah expressed her concerns about Mirah and the classroom environment, and about Jaime's inexperience, but Leah stated that she was pretty sure Rochelle could qualify based on her academic deficits alone. Delores decided to secure permission to test in both academics and behavior. For cognition, Delores used (a) WJ-III Cognitive, (b) Vineland II, and (c) WISC IV subtest: Matrix Reasoning. For academic skills, Delores used (a) results from KeyMath 3, and (b) WIAT-III. Delores also tested Rochelle's adaptive behavior using the Vineland Adaptive Scale, as well as parent, student, and teacher interviews. Results of these assessments can be found below.

Assessment Results

Rochelle speaks English at home and best expressed herself orally. Her receptive English is average compared to her peers, and her expressive English is slightly below average compared to her peers. The student is not limited English proficient.

Rochelle's vision is within normal limits without glasses. Her hearing is also within normal limits without aids. Rochelle's health history does not indicate any significant issues. She does not appear to have any physical conditions which directly affect her ability to profit from the educational process. Therefore, adapted physical education is not indicated.

Rochelle lives with her foster parents. She loves music, watching TV, and playing at the church. While she is overcoming her legacy of early abuse, Rochelle shows no concerns regarding cultural, linguistic, or experiential factors that influence her learning and behavioral patterns. She participated in Head Start and made good academic progress through third grade, so there is no lack of previous educational opportunities in reading and/or math.

Behavioral Observations

Behavioral observations from the foster parents indicate that Rochelle has emotional outbursts at home. She will cry, shout, and pout but eventually accept the limitation placed on her. She does have a change in eating habits if she is upset. When not in school, Rochelle enjoys music, playing at the church, and interacting with the family.

Behavioral observations from the classroom teacher indicate that Rochelle will pout and withdraw from the activity or group when she is upset. She also appears to have a short attention span for reading and math. It is difficult to keep her on task in large and small groups. Rochelle's teacher was asked to compare Rochelle (age 9 years and 2 months) to her peers, which generated the following results:

- Generally cooperates or is compliant with teacher request: **Average**
- Adapts to new situations without getting upset: **Average**
- Accepts responsibility for own actions: **Below Average**
- Makes and keep friends at school: **Average**
- Works cooperatively with others: **Average**
- Has an even and happy disposition: **Average**
- Is pleased with good work: **Average**
- Initiates activities independently: **Average**
- Responds appropriately to praise and correction: **Average**
- Resists becoming discouraged by difficulties and minor setbacks: **Poor**

While the teacher raises some behavioral concerns, Rochelle's behavior both in school and out of school does not appear to influence learning and education placement, programming, or discipline.

Intellectual and Behavioral Assessments

Rochelle's intellectual/behavioral assessments were conducted via a Cross Battery Assessment using the Cattell-Horn-Carroll (CHC) Theory of Cognitive Abilities. This approach bridges the current intellectual theory, and research and practice by reliably measuring a wider range of cognitive abilities/processes than presented by a single intelligence battery. It also offers a psychometrically defensible means to identify population-relative (i.e., normative) strengths and weaknesses in cognitive ability/processes.

Rochelle was cooperative throughout the testing process. She appeared at ease, comfortable and attentive. She responded slowly and carefully to test questions and persisted even when tasks became more difficult. Therefore, the test results are considered valid and reliable. Tables 4.2 - 4.5 contains Rochelle's results from the (a) Woodcock Johnson III, (b) KeyMath 3, (c) DIBELS, and (d) AIMSweb for Math. Table 4.6 provides Rochelle's report card grades.

Table 4.2 • Woodcock-Johnson III

Subtest	Composite Score	Percentile	Grade Equivalent	Level
GIA (EXT)	89	22%	2.6	Average/ Within Normal Limits
*Verbal Ability	104	60%	4.7	Average/ Within Normal Limits
**Thinking Ability	89	23%	2.4	Average/ Within Normal Limits
***Cognitive Efficiency	86	18%	2.8	Average/ Within Normal Limits
Comprehension - Knowledge	104	60%	4.7	Average/ Within Normal Limits
Long Term Retrieval	72	3%	1.4	Below Average/ Normative Weakness
Visual-Spatial Thinking	98	44%	3.7	Average/ Within Normal Limits
Auditory Processing	105	64%	6.1	Average/ Within Normal Limits
****Fluid Reasoning	80	9%	1.8	Below Average/ Normative Weakness
Processing Speed	95	38%	3.8	Average/ Within Normal Limits
Short-Term Memory	82	11%	1.7	Below Average/ Normative Weakness

Standardized results for the WJ-III are:

116-130 = Above Average/Normative Strength

85-115 = Average/Within Normal Limits

70-84 = Below Average/Normative Weakness

69 or below = Lower Extreme/Normative Weakness

*Verbal ability refers to breadth and depth of acquired knowledge, ability to communicate knowledge, ability to reason based on previous learning.

**Thinking ability refers to the ability to perceive, analyze, synthesize, think with visual patterns, ability to store and recall visual representations, and discriminate auditory information.

***Cognitive Efficiency refers to short-term memory and processing speed.

****Fluid Reasoning refers to mental operations used in a novel task that cannot be performed automatically.

Table 4.3 • KeyMath 3

Composite Test	Scaled Score	Grade Equivalent	Percentile	Level
Basic Concepts	72	1.7	3%	Below Average

Subtest	Scaled Score	Grade Equivalent	Notes (use this for your own personal notes)	
Numeration	4	1.4		
Algebra	5	1.8		
Geometry	7	2.2		
Measurement	7	2.4		
Data Analysis & Probability	3	K.5		

Composite Test	Scaled Score	Grade Equivalent	Percentile	Level
Operations	84	3.1	14%	Below Average

Subtest	Scaled Score	Grade Equivalent	Notes (use this for your own personal notes)	
Mental Computation & Estimation	5	2.1		
Addition & Subtraction	8	3.5		
Multiplication & Division	10	4.2		

Composite Test	Scaled Score	Grade Equivalent	Percentile	Level
Applications	73	1.8	4%	Below Average

Subtest	Scaled Score	Grade Equivalent	Notes (use this for your own personal notes)	
Foundations of Problem Solving	5	1.8		
Applied Problem Solving	5	1.5		

Composite Test	Scaled Score	Grade Equivalent	Percentile	Level
Total Test	72	2.2	5%	Below Average

Standard scores for the KeyMath 3 are:

Below 70 = Well-Below Average

70-85 = Below Average

85-115 = Average

115-130 = Above Average

Above 130 = Well-Above Average

Table 4.4 • DIBELS			
Test	**Score**	**Score Level**	**Notes** (use this for your own personal notes)
Composite Score	289	Below Benchmark	
DORF Words Correct	80	Below Benchmark	
DORF Accuracy	94	Below Benchmark	
Retell Fluency	20	Below Benchmark	

Score Goal Interpretation for beginning of school year

DIBELS Composite Score
  0-244 = Well Below Benchmark
  245-289 = Below Benchmark
  290-886 = At or Above Benchmark

DORF Words Correct
  0-69 = Well Below Benchmark
  70-89 = Below Benchmark
  90-350 = At or Above Benchmark

DORF Accuracy
  0-92 = Well Below Benchmark
  93-95 = Below Benchmark
  96-100 = At or Above Benchmark

Retell Fluency
  27-94 = Well Below Benchmark
  14-25 = Below Benchmark
  27-94 = At or Above Benchmark

Table 4.5 • AIMSweb for Math			
Subtest	**Score**	**Percentile**	**Level**
Computation and Application	4	Below 15%	Below Average
Computation	10	Below 15%	Below Average

Scale of performance levels for AIMSweb for Math are:
  11th-25th Percentile = Below Average
  26th-74th Percentile = Average
  75th-89th Percentile = Above Average
  90th-99th Percentile = Well-Above Average

Table 4.6 • Report Card Grades

Subject	Grade	Notes (use this for your own personal notes)
Reading	82	
Math	64	
Language Arts	80	
Science	88	
Social Studies	83	
Art	Exemplary	
Health	Exemplary	
PE	100	
Music	100	
Computer	100	

Rochelle was also administered the Vineland Adaptive Behavior Scales at age 9 years and 2 months. The results are found in Table 4.7

Table 4.7 • Vineland Adaptive Behavior Scales

Domain	Standard Score	Adaptive Level	Notes (use this for your own personal notes)
Daily Living Skills	95	Adequate	
Socialization	109	Adequate	
Adaptive Behavior Composite	105	Adequate	

Standardized results for the Vineland Adaptive Behavior Scales are:

130-140 = High Adaptive Level

115-129 = Moderately High Adaptive Level

86-114 = Adequate Adaptive Level

71-85 = Moderately Low Adaptive Level

20-70 = Low Adaptive Level

Rochelle was administered the Wechsler Intelligence Scale for Children IV and the Wechsler Individual Achievement Test Third Edition at age 9 years and 2 months, which generated the results found in Table 4.8.

Subtest	Composite Score	Percentile	Grade Equivalent	Level
Word Reading	102	55%	4.7	Average
Reading Comprehension	91	27%	2.8	Average
Pseudoword Decoding	110	75%	6.0	High Average
Numerical Operations	101	53%	4.4	Average
Math Reasoning	76	5%	2.2	Borderline
Written Expression	95	37%	3.2	Average
*Matrix Reasoning = 70				Borderline/ Below Average

Table 4.8 • Wechsler Individual Achievement Test Second Edition

*Matrix Reasoning (based on results from WISC-IV) refers to the ability to use logic and solve a problem.

Standardized results for the WISC-IV are:

146-159 = Highly Gifted

130-145 = Moderately Gifted

120-129 = Above Average

110-119 = High Average

90-109 = Average

80-89 = Low Average

70-79 = Borderline/Below Average

Standard scores for the WIAT-III are:

Below 70 = Extremely Low

70-79 = Borderline

80-89 = Low Average

90-109 = Average

110-119 = High Average

120-129 = Superior

Above 130 = Very Superior

Your Task

You are now familiar with Rochelle's background and her current strengths and weaknesses. You have also met her multidisciplinary team which consists of Mirah, Leah, Delores, Jaime, and Aisha. The team has considered Delores' testing results,

Topics for Discussion:
Grade Inflation

the data Mirah and Jaime collected, and Aisha's concerns. The team has decided that Rochelle qualifies for special education services. Your task is as follows:

1. Determine Rochelle's qualifying disability.

2. Assume the role of Leah, as she will be the primary developer of any IEP that is written. Utilizing your state's IEP form, develop an appropriate IEP for Rochelle. You will want to complete *all* relevant sections of the IEP.

Things to consider:

- Rochelle's primary disabling condition
- Rochelle's required services
- Who provides the services and where
- Positive behavior development in Rochelle

IEP Resources

Anatomy of an IEP – www.understood.org (find the search bar and type in "Anatomy of an IEP")

Hedin, L., & DeSpain, H. (2018). SMART or not? Writing specific, measurable goals. *Teaching Exceptional Children, 51*(2), 100-110.

IRIS Center IEP Module – www.iris.peabody.vanderbilt.edu (click on Resources > IRS Resource Locator > IEPs > Modules)

National Association of Special Education Teachers – www.naset.org (type in "Completed Sample IEP" in the search bar and click on the first link provided)

U. S. Department of Education – www2.ed.gov/parents/landing.jhtml (type "IEP", into the search bar and click on top link which says Archived: Guide to the IEP, Click 15, Sample form)

Figure 4.2. Individualized Education Plan Resources

References

Individuals with Disabilities Education Improvement Act, 20 U.S.C. § 1400 (2004).

Jung, L. A. (2007). Writing SMART objectives and strategies that fit the ROUTINE. *Teaching Exceptional Children, 39*(4), 54-58.

CHAPTER 5

Rochelle Needs Behavior Support: Writing Behavior Intervention Plans

This chapter provides a description of Rochelle's escalating behavior at school and a description of the components of a Functional Behavioral Assessment (FBA) and a Behavior Intervention Plan (BIP). Please note that states differ in their terminology so for this chapter, the BIP is the same thing as a Behavior Support Plan. After reading the required FBA and BIP components, a case study will be provided which can be used to write an FBA and/or BIP. As you consider BIPs, keep these questions in mind:

- What is the purpose of a BIP?
- What is a target behavior?
- What is the purpose of identifying the function of a student's behavior?

Discussion of Behavior Intervention Plans

This section provides background information on the parts of a Functional Behavioral Assessment (FBA) and Behavior Intervention Plan (BIP) and will help in writing these documents for any student with an identified problem behavior. The Individuals with Disabilities Education Improvement Act (IDEIA; 2004) does not provide much guidance in the area of FBAs and BIPs. However, it does state that schools must address behavior concerns in a proactive manner and document the behavior in the IEP. FBAs and BIPs should be written by members of the IEP team who know the student. All team members should play an essential role in gathering data for the FBA and the BIP; however, the special education teacher or someone else well versed in behavior should take the lead.

Definition

IDEIA (2004) does not specifically define FBAs or BIPs in the mandates, but it emphasizes the importance of when to conduct an FBA and develop a BIP. IDEIA also discusses the requirement of students receiving a Free and Appropriate Public Education (FAPE) and that they be educated in the Least Restrictive Environment (LRE). This is important to consider because behavior problems can lead to a student being isolated or removed from their regular placement. Ultimately, to follow the IDEIA mandates, FBAs and BIPs should be conducted when the student's behavior impacts their access to classroom-based education, and/or their behavior impacts least restrictive environment.

A BIP outlines a student's target behavior, the replacement behavior, and the strategies to be used when working with a student. The BIP should be written in a proactive and positive manner. Good practice would be basing the behavior plan off the results of an FBA; however, this is not always done. Furthermore, the BIP should be followed and documented before taking any disciplinary measures on a student.

Purpose

FBAs should be conducted on students when behavior is of concern. FBAs determine the function of a student's targeted behavior. Knowing the function of the student's behavior will help teachers and interventionists determine appropriate strategies to change the targeted behavior. IDEIA also requires an FBA when a student has a disciplinary change of placement. In other words, they are out of placement for more than 10 days *or* when a Manifestation Determination Review (MDR) has been conducted and the behavior in question is due to the child's disability. It is also highly recommended to complete an FBA on any student who has a BIP. How can you create effective interventions if you do not know why a student is behaving the way they are?

The FBA data allows the team to make informed decisions when creating a BIP. BIPs are required for any student whose behavior interferes with their learning or the learning of other students. The purpose of the BIP is to provide stakeholders with the interventions necessary to change the student's targeted behavior. The BIP is similar to the goals, objectives and the accommodations part of the IEP. Anyone working with the student should know the targeted behavior, replacement behaviors, function of the behavior, and the interventions to be used when working with the student.

Necessary Legal Components

There are several components necessary to develop a quality, legally defensible FBA and BIP (IRIS Center, 2009). Behavior is subjective in nature, so you want to be as scientific as possible, and it is important to have administrator support for your plan. The key pieces of FBAs and BIPs are addressed below with a brief explanation. The IRIS Center also provides a more detailed look into the FBA process, including writing a behavior plan. It is important that you research your specific state and/or district regulations related to these concepts.

- **Functional Behavioral Assessment**
  - Target behavior
    - FBAs are conducted on any behavior(s) that the school staff and/or parents deem as negatively impacting the educational performance of the student. These become known as the target behavior(s).
    - There are two types of behavior – externalizing and internalizing.
      * *Externalizing* behaviors are those easily observable and cause disruption in the classroom (e.g., throwing things, verbal outbursts).
      * *Internalizing* behaviors are those that do not cause major disruption during the school day and often are undiagnosed (e.g., depression, sleeping in class, not paying attention/daydreaming).
    - When writing target behaviors, it is important they are written in observable and measurable terms.
      * Incorrect Example: *Gabrielle is disruptive in math class.* This does not tell the reader what she is doing. What exactly is disruptive? What is disruptive to me may not be considered disruptive by other students or teachers.
      * Correct Example: *As soon as independent work is assigned, Gabrielle is up out of her seat walking around the classroom talking to other students.* The reader now knows when the behavior occurs and what Gabrielle is doing that is considered disruptive by the teacher.
  - Sources of information/data collection
    - After identifying the target behavior, the next step is to collect quality data from multiple sources. There are two types of data collection: indirect and direct.
    - **Indirect data collection** is completed without specifically observing a student's behavior. This data includes reviewing school records and interviewing the family, student, and teachers. Many interview forms can be found with a simple Google search.
    - **Direct data collection** occurs when the student's behavior is witnessed and documented. This type of data includes: (a) frequency or event recording, (b) interval recording, (c) duration recording, (d) latency recording, and (e) product samples. The IRIS Center independent activities are an excellent resource for more practice with data collection.
      * *Frequency or Event Recording* is used to determine the number of times a student engages in the target behavior during a specific time period. This type of data collection is used for behaviors that have a distinct beginning and end.

◊ *Example:* Ang does not raise his hand to ask a question, but instead blurts out his questions during direct instruction.

* *Interval Recording* is used when it is difficult to count the specific number of instances, such as for behaviors that occur several times within a set time period. Interval recording is used to measure the occurrence of the target behavior within a pre-determined time limit.

◊ *Example:* The teacher will record whether or not Kiran is working on his independent assignment every five minutes.

* *Duration recording* is used to determine how long the targeted behavior lasts.

◊ *Example:* The teacher will record how long Dara cries when she is not permitted to choose a reward from the prize box.

* *Latency recording* is used to determine the amount of time that passes between a given request and behavior compliance.

◊ *Example:* The behavior interventionist will record how long it takes Adam to begin his math assignment after the teacher provides instruction to begin.

* When collecting baseline and intervention data, it is recommended the observations take place at the same time under the same conditions. The baseline data should include at least five observational sessions. Be consistent with your data collection.

* Graph both the baseline and intervention data so the IEP team can easily see the changes between the baseline and intervention data. Graphing the baseline data also helps provide specific information on the severity of the target behavior.

▪ A-B-C Chart

* Predictors and consequences of behavior can be found by completing an A-B-C chart.

* *Antecedent*: The action occurring immediately before the student engages in the target behavior.

◊ *Example* - Mrs. Smith passes out a math worksheet to be completed independently.

* *Behavior*: The student's action that occurs during the observation period.

◊ *Example*: Shawna rips up her math worksheet and throws it in the trash.

          * Consequence: The action occurring immediately after the student engages in the target behavior.

            ◊ *Example:* Mrs. Smith tells Shawna to leave the classroom.

- When collecting data for an FBA, including an A-B-C chart with the direct and indirect assessment is recommended.

○ Function of Behavior/Hypothesis Statement

- All behavior serves a function. There are three functions or purposes of behaviors: (a) to gain attention or a tangible reward, (b) to avoid or escape something, and (c) gain power or control over themselves or a situation by manipulating sensory input.

- Knowing the function of the target behavior and having quality data will assist in writing a hypothesis statement.

      * *Example:* The function of Gianna's disruptive behavior, which includes talking out of turn and roaming the classroom, stems from Gianna seeking attention of the classroom teacher. This is evidenced by the data collected showing that Gianna only engages in this behavior during independent work time. This behavior is reinforced by the teacher when she responds saying things like, "Gianna, please sit down and do your work quietly."

- Once the hypothesis statement is developed, identification of replacement behaviors and effective interventions can be identified in the BIP.

- **Behavior Intervention Plans**

○ When writing a BIP, goals should be observable and measurable.

- As a quick reminder (from Chapter 2), goals should follow the SMART or LBCC criteria. Your goal should include: **L** - the **Learner** mentioned by name, **B** – specific and observable behavior, **C** - the condition needed to perform the behavior, and **C** - the criteria to demonstrate mastery.

- Remember, behavior goals should be based on the data collected in the FBA.

○ Understanding if a behavior is an actual *behavioral issue* (they won't do it or lack the skills to do it) **or** if it is an *academic issue* (they can't do it) is necessary when developing interventions.

- If the behavior is a result of the student being unable to complete the task, then the team needs to look at academic interventions to help the student.

- If the student is knowingly misbehaving or they do not possess the skills to behave appropriately, then it is likely an actual behavior issue that needs to be addressed in a behavior plan.
- Another aspect of behavior plans that is oftentimes overlooked is the evaluation. Ongoing data collection should occur, as it is the only way to determine if the behavior plan is still working and relevant for the student. Ongoing data collection will reveal if the BIP is ineffective or if the student demonstrates mastery. This will help determine if a BIP needs to be revised or rewritten.
- Many times, the person responsible for implementing the BIP does not need to be the special education teacher. The person or people responsible for implementing the BIP can be anyone who works with the student. This could be a counselor, a paraprofessional, a preferred adult, or even the cafeteria worker. The person responsible should be able to reinforce the student in the exact situation and at the same time the behavior occurs.
  - *Example:* Maksim picks up a piece of trash off the floor, and the custodian positively reinforces him by saying, "Thank you so much for helping me pick up that trash."
- Replacement Behavior
  - A replacement behavior is any behavior that can take the place of the target behavior and achieve the desired reinforcement.
  - The replacement behavior should be chosen after determining the function of the target behavior and writing the hypothesis statement. The hypothesis is validated because the replacement behavior resulted in the desired reinforcement.
  - Replacement behaviors should be culturally and socially acceptable.
    * *Example*: When teaching Lindsay to wait patiently for the bus, instead of hitting when frustrated she can flip through an age-appropriate magazine of her interest.
  - Replacement behaviors should be written in observable and measurable terms.
- Environmental accommodations can be very useful when intervening with antecedents. Often, making changes within the environment can positively impact the target behavior.
  - *Example:* If a student with autism is sensitive to overhead lighting, dimming the lights might prevent the problem behavior from occurring.

- If the applied environmental accommodation prevents the student from engaging in the problem behavior, then a behavior plan may be unnecessary.

○ Reinforcement strategies are useful when addressing consequences. Finding ways to positively reinforce a student for demonstrating the appropriate behavior may be the only change needed to decrease the targeted behavior. When altering the applied reinforcement strategy results in positive behavior, the behavior plan may be unnecessary. However, it is possible the perceived consequences may elicit continued behavior problems. Examples below are for a student who is seeking attention.

  - *Example:* If LaShonda raises her hand to ask a question, and the teacher says "Thank you for raising your hand LaShonda. What is your question?" LaShonda is more likely to repeat the appropriate behavior.

  - *Example:* If LaShonda makes a rude sound while the teacher is leading instruction and her peers laugh, she is highly likely to repeat the offending sound.

○ Key components of a behavior plan are the interventions. There are many interventions that can be used in BIPs, and they should be based on the specific behavior and the individual student. Figure 5.1 on page 50 contains a list of resources that can be used to locate more information on behavioral interventions.

Legal Considerations

Behavior problems present unique legal challenges for students with disabilities. This section provides an overview of the most significant legal considerations for special education students as they relate to creating behavior plans. It is vital to consult your state and district guidelines regarding student behavior because this area is highly litigious.

Topic(s) for Discussion: *State guidelines for conducting FBAs and writing BIPs.*

Least Restrictive Environment

Least restrictive environment (LRE) is the concept that individuals with disabilities will be educated with their non-disabled peers to the maximum extent possible. When patterns of student removal due to behaviors are identified, the team must address the behavior in question in the IEP. Additionally, when a student with a

Figure 5.1. Behavior Strategy Resources

disability violates the student code of conduct the IEP team needs to reconvene to address these behaviors. Anytime you remove a student with a disabling condition from their general education setting, you must justify that decision and specifically state how much time that student will be away from their non-disabled peers.

Manifestation Determination Review (MDR)

One question that arises when educating students with challenging behaviors is, "What do we do when the student breaks the student code of conduct?" Ultimately, if a student breaks the student code of conduct then a consequence is given. Many times, the student receives an out-of-school suspension. The purpose

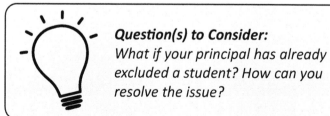

Question(s) to Consider:
What if your principal has already excluded a student? How can you resolve the issue?

of the Manifestation Determination Review (MDR) is to evaluate the data and determine if the behavior in question is a direct result of the disability. MDR procedures are specific, so relying on the district special education psychologist or diagnostician will be important to ensure that the student's rights are protected. It is also vital that each stakeholder involved in the MDR proceedings remain focused on responding to the required questions and not assigning arbitrary value to the behavior displayed.

Time-Out, Seclusion, and Restraint

There are other ways students are removed from participation with their non-disabled peers, especially in response to behavioral issues. Some schools may use time-out, seclusion or restraint. Time-out, seclusion and restraints are only to be used when a student is in immediate and serious danger to themselves or others. These are used as a last resort, and documentation in the IEP is required. The United States Department of Education website (www2.ed.gov) provides a resource titled *Restraint and Seclusion: Resource Document,* which provides information regarding seclusion and restraint by state and territory.

Time-Out

According to Wolf, McLaughlin, and Williams (2006), time-out is a behavioral technique used to decrease the frequency of a student's target behavior. Removing a student into a setting to help them calm down, only when approved, is considered time-out (CRDC, 2010, as cited in USDE, 2012). The use of time-out is a controversial topic that should only be used as a last resort. Most importantly, educators need to remember that if time-out will be used, it *must* be documented in a student's IEP. Ensure you follow your state and district guidelines when thinking about the use of time-out procedures.

Seclusion

The Civil Rights Data Collection (as cited in USDE, 2012) defines seclusion as:

> The involuntary confinement of a student alone in a room or area from which the student is physically prevented from leaving. It does not include timeout, which is a behavior management technique that is part of an approved program, involves the monitored separation of the student in a non-locked setting, and is implemented for the purpose of calming. (p. 10).

Implementing seclusion procedures will vary by state and district. Always check with your administrators before using a seclusion technique. You will also want to remember to clearly document the use of seclusion in the IEP.

Restraint

According to the Civil Rights Data Collection (as cited in USDE, 2012), there are two types of restraints: physical and mechanical. The CRDC (as cited in USDE, 2012) defines physical restraints as:

> A personal restriction that immobilizes or reduces the ability of a student to move his or her torso, arms, legs, or head freely. The term physical restraint does not include a physical escort. Physical escort means a temporary touching or holding of the hand, wrist, arm, shoulder, or back for the purpose of inducing a student who is acting out to walk to a safe location. (p. 10).

CRDC defines mechanical restraints as:

> The use of any device or equipment to restrict a student's freedom of movement. This term does not include devices implemented by trained school personnel, or utilized by a student that have been prescribed by an appropriate medical or related services professional and are used for the specific and approved purposes for which such devices were designed, such as: Adaptive devices or mechanical supports used to achieve proper body position, balance, or alignment to allow greater freedom of mobility than would be possible without the use of such devices or mechanical supports; Vehicle safety restraints when used as intended during the transport of a student in a moving vehicle; Restraints for medical immobilization; or Orthopedically prescribed devices that permit a student to participate in activities without risk of harm. (p. 10).

Check with your district administrators before using restraints on a student. Restraints should only be used by staff who are properly trained in non-violent crisis intervention techniques. Documentation of regular restraint use must be identified as an intervention in the IEP. Restraint can be used in an emergency without documentation in the IEP; however, all restraints must be documented on the appropriate district/state forms, and the parents must be notified. Even in an emergency, all staff involved must be properly trained.

Case Study

As you read the case study, consider the following key questions:

- What is Rochelle's target behavior?
- What is the function of Rochelle's behavior?
- What strategies/interventions can be used to help improve Rochelle's target behavior?

Rochelle has successfully completed elementary school and met all her IEP goals. She is reading and doing math on grade level, and her behavior from the IFSP has improved considerably. She only occasionally refuses to comply with a teacher demand, and she can be re-directed easily. With Aisha's guidance, Rochelle is doing very well on the piano, and participated in several school music events, singing and playing the recorder. Music is Rochelle's favorite subject. She is doing much better at home and developed a good relationship with DeMarcas.

Rochelle started sixth grade in the middle school. Her middle school special education teacher, Timothy, has been teaching for five years. He spent 10 years in the military before being honorably discharged and becoming a teacher. He enjoys working with middle school-age children and loves helping them improve their academics and behavior. He is considered strict, and his no-nonsense style seems to work with most of his students.

Timothy works closely with the middle school counselor to ensure that Rochelle keeps music as part of her daily schedule. He also wants to include Rochelle in his co-taught sections of English and math to keep an eye on her. He is concerned that the amount of chaos in the hallways, particularly when changing classes, may overwhelm Rochelle. Timothy knows from experience that many of his sixth graders struggle in the first month to get organized and get to the right class on time. He is grateful the district made the decision to do away with lockers and textbooks. Now in middle school, each child is issued a laptop that they use for the rest of middle and high school. Teachers give them access to textbooks online, and all their work is submitted through the computer. However, this too has been a struggle for some of Timothy's students, and he keeps a close eye on his sixth graders in particular. Since Rochelle does not appear to have any intellectual disabilities, Timothy is less concerned about her ability to use the technology and more about her learning *how* to use it. As a result, he recommends that Rochelle does not need assistive technology as much as she will need a check-in/check-out system to ensure that she knows how to use her laptop. Timothy recommends placing Rochelle in his homeroom each morning to check in, and in his co-taught Math class during the last period of the day so he can help Rochelle get ready for the evening's homework.

Rochelle's transition to sixth grade went smoothly for the first couple weeks. Timothy kept a close eye on Rochelle, frequently checking in with her to ensure that she was getting to her classes on time and keeping up with her supplies. He gradually tapered off his frequent checks, and now just quickly chats with her during her morning and afternoon check in/check out times.

Michelle, the band teacher, is thrilled with Rochelle's progress. Rochelle has quickly become a star music student. It is obvious to both Michelle and Aisha, Rochelle's foster mom, that Rochelle is a gifted musician, and both have been encouraging her to work harder and explore more in music. Michelle has started

Rochelle on several instruments, but Rochelle's favorite is the saxophone. Rochelle is regularly featured in performances.

Academically, Rochelle maintains a high C average in language arts, science, and social studies. She still struggles with reading comprehension, particularly in textbooks, and often requires Timothy's help to understand in class. However, Rochelle maintains a high B average in Math. She demonstrates progress toward mastering her IEP goals, and Timothy is very satisfied with her academic progress. He has noticed, however, that Rochelle has trouble staying organized. She often misses assignments or pieces of assignments and cannot remember where she saved documents in her school-issued laptop. She struggles to complete multi-step projects, and she often misses parts of instruction because she is distracted in class. She has difficulty concentrating on her work when others are present, so Rochelle's teachers have started sending her to the library or Timothy's classroom to complete her independent work.

While Rochelle is doing well in school, things are not going so well at home. Aisha and DeMarcas have also noticed that Rochelle is highly distracted, often beginning but not completing her chores, or even getting up in the middle of a television show to do something else. In addition, Rochelle began a relationship with Xavier, a boy she met at DeMarcas' church. Rochelle is now 13, and Xavier is 15. Xavier participates in the mentorship program DeMarcas sponsors at the high school. Aisha was not happy about the relationship and warned Rochelle to be careful. Aisha and DeMarcas suspect that even though Xavier claims to not belong to the gang his older brother joined, he may in fact be participating. DeMarcas has set very clear boundaries on the relationship stating that Rochelle cannot go anywhere with Xavier unsupervised. Most of the time, Xavier comes to Rochelle's house and spends time with her there or at church activities.

In October, the Middle School will host a homecoming dance. It is the first opportunity for Rochelle to attend a real dance with her peers and her new boyfriend. Aisha spent a great deal of time talking with Rochelle about behaving appropriately in that environment, particularly with Xavier. DeMarcas and Randall, Rochelle's brother, helped Rochelle work on her dance moves, and Aisha took Rochelle shopping for a new dress. Randall, who is now in the eighth grade, will also attend the dance, and he informed Rochelle that she had to stay with the other "little kids" and not bother him at the dance.

After the homecoming dance, Rochelle's relationship with Xavier became contentious. The cycle of breaking up and getting back together seemed never ending. Rochelle became moody and even more distracted at home. Aisha had difficulty redirecting her tasks, and she noticed that Rochelle changed the way she dressed. She was always in long sleeves, mostly hoodies and leggings, even when the weather was warm. At school, Rochelle's grades began to slip. Where she had high C's, she was now earning D's and F's. Her math grade slipped to a D as well.

One afternoon, Aisha and DeMarcas were called to the school. When they arrived, John, the principal, explained that there was a problem with Rochelle. Rochelle was marked present for her first class of the day. When the teacher told her to get her head off the desk and pay attention, she told the teacher to "go ***** yourself." The teacher sent Rochelle to the principal's office. After class, the teacher came to the office to bring the discipline referral, but no one in the office had seen Rochelle. She was marked absent in her next two classes. John called in Officer Miles, the School Resource Officer, and they went through the security camera footage. They saw Rochelle leave the main campus through a side door, sneak through an opening in the fence, and walk down the sidewalk. Officer Miles called the city police to begin a search.

Four hours later, Rochelle was found with Xavier. Officer Miles brought Rochelle home where Aisha and DeMarcas were frantically waiting. Rochelle sobbed when they walked in and threw herself into Aisha's arms. She kept saying that she was so sorry. She never meant any harm. She didn't want to be in trouble. Officer Miles explained that Xavier had been arrested on multiple charges related to gang activity.

In the chaos, the sleeve of Rochelle's jacket pulled up her arm. Aisha immediately noticed cuts on her wrist and in the bend of her elbow. She grabbed Rochelle's arm and asked her how she got the cuts. Rochelle quickly pulled her arm away, covered it with her sleeve, and said they were accidents. Officer Miles asked Rochelle if Xavier had cut her, and Rochelle was adamant that Xavier had never hurt her physically. DeMarcas asked Rochelle if she had done this to herself. Rochelle started crying again and refused to answer. Officer Miles took pictures of the injuries and added them to his report to the Middle School.

Stakeholder Perspectives

For most adolescents with behavior issues, there are several stakeholders involved with the student. Each stakeholder has a unique perspective on the student, and all those perspectives are important to build an accurate picture of the student's needs. Sometimes, personal agendas can also be identified in a stakeholder's perspective, so IEP teams need to be aware of bias that may exist.

Topic(s) for Discussion:
Stakeholder bias and its impact on programming

While not inherently bad or wrong, bias can influence the outcomes of an MDR or BIP. Stakeholders may need to have a professional and frank discussion about what is best for the student.

Foster Parent Concerns

Aisha and DeMarcas are at a loss for how to intervene with Rochelle. They thought they had monitored her behavior closely and carefully guided her through this relationship with Xavier. They continued to notice Rochelle's highly distractible behavior. Several weeks before the incident at school, Aisha took Rochelle to their family doctor who recommended an evaluation for Attention Deficit/Hyperactivity Disorder. Aisha has an appointment scheduled for the evaluation, but she is unsure if she should pursue it with so many other issues right now. Aisha contacted Amanda, Rochelle's social worker, right away to tell her about the school incident. Amanda came to the house that evening to discuss the situation with Aisha, DeMarcas, and Rochelle.

Social Worker Concerns

Amanda was shocked at the turn of events for Rochelle. She dropped all her other work to have a home visit immediately. Amanda took the Rochelle and Randall case very personally. She had been with them since their placement in foster care, and she fought hard to remain with them all this time. They are her "poster children" that the system can work. She refused to let them be anything less than successful.

When she arrived at the home of Aisha and DeMarcas, the house was unusually quiet. The first thing Amanda noticed is that there was no music playing. There was no food out either. Aisha always offered some type of homemade treat, and DeMarcas made the best coffee she had ever tasted, but none of that happened this evening. Amanda knew then it was bad.

Amanda listened quietly and carefully, taking notes, while DeMarcas explained what happened that day. Aisha cried quietly. Randall played a game on his phone, pretending not to hear what was being said. Rochelle sat in silence on the couch with a hoodie pulled over her head. Amanda was shocked yet again when DeMarcas showed her the printouts of the injuries on Rochelle's arm. Amanda asked Rochelle to see her arm. Rochelle told Amanda, "Bite me."

For the first time that evening, Randall spoke up. He said, "She won't show you. She's been doing it for a while now. You should see her stomach." Rochelle jumped up off the couch and ran to Randall. She began hitting him with a pillow, screaming, "You promised not to tell!" DeMarcas pulled Rochelle off Randall and guided her back to the couch. He then went to Randall, knelt before him, and said, "You did the right thing. Your sister is in trouble. You did the right thing." Amanda said, "I'm proud of you, Randall." Randall was then dismissed to his room.

Amanda told Rochelle to show her arm and stomach. Rochelle finally agreed displaying the fresh cuts on her arm, and what appeared to be old burn marks on her stomach. Aisha cried harder. Amanda took photos to document the marks. Amanda then asked, "Did you do this to yourself or did someone do this to you?" Rochelle refused to answer. Amanda stated, "Rochelle, if you do not talk to me, I have to assume someone is hurting you. I have to assume it could be someone in this house. That means I might have to find a new home for you. I need the truth." Rochelle finally murmured that she had done it to herself.

Amanda is not unfamiliar with self-harm in teenagers. Given the circumstances, it made sense. She knows that they are facing two primary issues. First, they must deal with Rochelle's obvious mental distress and self-injurious behaviors. Second, they must sort out the issues at school causing her to fail. Amanda recommended that Aisha or DeMarcas accompany her to the emergency room for Rochelle's condition to be evaluated. DeMarcas and Amanda left with Rochelle.

Administrator Concerns

John spoke with Officer Miles the night of the incident. He was relieved that Xavier was now a freshman and no longer on his campus, and he was furious that Rochelle had left campus to be with him. He was also frustrated that he was just now being told about the academic failures and behavior issues Rochelle was having. John spoke with DeMarcas on the phone that night as well. DeMarcas tried to explain Rochelle's side of the situation, including the discovery of self-harm, but John assured DeMarcas that some type of disciplinary action would take place. When John returned to school the next morning, he re-

Question(s) to Consider:
Is this decision to place Rochelle in In School Suspension violating her least restrictive environment (LRE)?

searched the student handbook and code of conduct. He listed several violations he felt Rochelle made:

1. *Disregard for authority:* Students shall not leave school grounds or school-sponsored events without permission.

2. *Disregard for authority:* Students shall not refuse to accept discipline management techniques assigned by a teacher or principal.

3. *Mistreatment of others:* Students shall not use profanity or vulgar language or make obscene gestures.

4. *Mistreatment of others:* Students shall not threaten a district student, employee, or volunteer, including off school property, if the conduct causes a substantial disruption to the educational environment.

He then began the paperwork to place Rochelle in In-School Suspension (ISS).

In looking up Rochelle's information, he noticed that she was in special education. This would complicate matters, but he was certain he could still take disciplinary action. He notified Timothy via email that the paperwork was coming.

Special Education Teacher Concerns

Timothy received John's email early that morning before he arrived on campus. He knew John was unsympathetic to his students, but this blindsided him. He was working with Aisha and DeMarcas to get the evaluation for ADHD completed, but he was shocked to hear about Rochelle's incident. He tracked down Officer Miles as soon as he arrived on campus to get the full story. He was now even more shocked to hear that the principal intended to take disciplinary action against Rochelle instead of convening the IEP committee. Timothy made the decision to contact Becky, the behavior specialist, directly.

Behavior Specialist Concerns

Although Becky had only been at this school for one academic year, she has a long history of working with individuals with challenging behaviors. She is highly educated and experienced. Becky believes that a good FBA leads to a good BIP, and that is the combination for positive results. She takes her time to carefully document the antecedents, behavior and consequences, and she never jumps to a conclusion. She and John often have conflict because of her slow, methodical approach.

When Becky received Timothy's call, she immediately began the documentation process. She directed Timothy to let John know she would be on campus this morning. She also sent John an email to confirm. In addition, she told Timothy to make Rochelle available for an interview.

After the contentious visit with John, and a reluctant interview late in the afternoon with Rochelle and Aisha, Becky knew more evaluation was required. John placed Rochelle in ISS and reluctantly allowed Becky to interview her. She informed John that she and any related services personnel would need

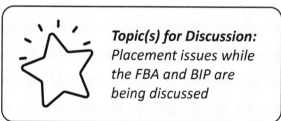

Topic(s) for Discussion: Placement issues while the FBA and BIP are being discussed

access to Rochelle, so they would have to meet on campus occasionally during Rochelle's time in ISS.

General Education Teacher Concerns

Music Teacher Concerns

Michelle just could not believe the news about Rochelle when Timothy shared it with her the following day. She assured Timothy that she would readily participate in any IEP meeting necessary. Michelle felt helpless in the situation until Becky contacted her for a functional interview. Michelle was relieved there was something, finally, that she could do to help Rochelle.

Assessment Results

Behavioral Observations

Physician's reports: Aisha provided these to Becky. The family practitioner had recommended an evaluation for ADHD. She was also concerned that Rochelle displayed symptoms of premenstrual dysphoric disorder (PMDD) and recommended that Rochelle begin medication to regulate her hormones. Otherwise, Rochelle was noted to be healthy and developmentally fit, although she was in the low-normal range for height and weight.

The attending ER physician evaluated Rochelle thoroughly. She found cuts that looked to be no more than three days old on Rochelle's left wrist and inner elbow. She also found what appeared to be a self-inflicted burn mark on the left side of her lower abdomen. Rochelle would not disclose how the marks were obtained. The attending psychiatrist was brought in, and he determined that while Rochelle was not suicidal, the self-harm indicated a pattern of psychological distress requiring intervention. He referred Amanda and DeMarcas to take Rochelle to see a psychiatrist as soon as possible. Becky knew from experience that there were only four licensed child and adolescent psychiatrists in the city, and the average wait time for an emergency appointment was three months.

Behavioral Assessments

Becky's Reports: Becky used several sources of information to determine the function of Rochelle's behavior. Due to time constraints and Rochelle's placement in ISS, Becky was unable to obtain observational data. Tables 5.1. and 5.2 on the next two pages provide a summary of the information Becky received while conducting functional interviews with each of Rochelle's teachers.

Table 5.1 • Teacher Interview Summary #1

	Manny (Science)	Natosha (Math)	Jonah (Physical Education)
Question #1: What do you see as Rochelle's strengths?	Peers seem to like her	When she turns work in, generally she does a good job	She always participates. She seems to be well liked by the other students Easily redirected
Question #2: What are the most concerning problem behaviors you are seeing with Rochelle?	Missing and late assignment Sleeping in class Making rude comments Tardy to class	Late to class Missing assignments Sleeping a lot Most recently has begun using vulgar language	She tends to chat a lot instead of focusing on the activity, so sometimes she gets distracted
Question #3: How often are each of these behaviors occurring and causing issues in class?	Multiple times per week, at least one of these every day	Multiple times per week (Late to class) I have lost count of zeroes (Missing assignments) Almost every day her head is being put down (Sleeping a lot) We have had two incidents since Mid-October (Vulgar language)	I usually have to bring her back (attention) every day Depends on how engaging the activity is will depend on how many times in a class period (Redirection)
Question #4: How do you manage Rochelle's behaviors?	I have told that girl, so many times, what the expectations are Stand in hall to get her to class on time (Tardies)	Reported tardies and talked to her about them Talked to Timothy and made sure to put a note so her parents could see it (Missing assignments) I say her name to redirect her and that is when she curses at me (Vulgar language)	I just call her name and remind her what she should be doing (Distractibility)
Question #5: How does Rochelle respond?	Ignores me Avoids me while I am standing in the hallway	Ignores me - continues to be tardy Uses vulgar language and walks out of class	She will say "Oh, ok" and gets back on task (Distractibility)

	Michelle (Band)	Joyce (Language Arts/ Reading)	Raavi (History)
Table 5.2 • Teacher Interview Summary #2			
Question #1: What do you see as Rochelle's strengths?	Gifted musician Very engaged	Even though she struggles with reading, she generally tries to do her work	She does her best work when she works in groups
Question #2: What are the most concerning problem behaviors you are seeing with Rochelle?	Occasionally distracted - turns around, looks at other students if she hears other students, If I work with a small group, she has difficulty independently practicing music	She has started sleeping in class, she puts her head on her desk and puts hoodie over her head - so I think she is asleep If I try to get her to wake up she will say things like "I don't care, this is stupid, this doesn't matter"	If she is not interested, she puts her head down Frequently makes comments of the subject such as "well he was stupid" When she puts her head down she seems to tune me out and then does not get her work done. In the last few weeks I have only gotten assignments from her when they are working in groups
Question #3: How often are each of these behaviors occurring and causing issues in class?	A couple of times each week - Mondays when we are getting started - Friday mornings after football games on Thursday night	Daily (Disrupting class) - Everyone sees her and they think they can do it too - it gets everyone off target	Daily
Question #4: How do you manage Rochelle's behaviors?	I generally just say her name and she gets back on target	I try to say her name to get her back, but when she puts her head back down there is nothing I can do I remind her take notes and do her assignments to get her grades back up because she is failing	I try to ignore them - she continues to not do anything
Question #5: How does Rochelle respond?	She usually gets right back on track - sometimes I usually have to say her name twice	Sometimes she will roll her eyes (Redirection) She used to get back on target and the last few weeks she just puts her head back down - it just seems to be a steady decline since October	She does not do her work

Below are examples of functional interviews that Becky completed with Rochelle, Aisha, and Michelle. The transcript of Becky's interview with Michelle is provided as an example of a functional interview with a teacher. Any additional data you would need from her other teachers can be found in the tables on the two previous pages.

Student Interview with Rochelle

Q: Is there anything that is happening outside of school lately that bothers you?
A: All this mess with Xavier. I don't understand why people are being so hard on him. He was just trying to help his brother.

Q: Is there something new that is happening to you?
A: Yeah. You know. That's why I have to talk to you.

Q: What is happening to you?
A: Why should I tell you what you already know! You know I'm in trouble because of wanting to be with Xavier and, you know, telling my teachers the truth! Who gives a shit about all that history and literature and crap?

Q: Who put the cuts on your arms?
A: [No answer]

Q: All right. Does it bother you that you are in trouble?
A: Yes, it bothers me! I don't want people mad at me. I don't like being in ISS all day. It's boring. Aisha won't let me out of her sight so I have to clean the church while she works. And she checks on me all the time! Even when I'm in bed! And I can't even listen to my music!

Q: Did you know it was against school rules to leave school?
A: I mean, I figured it might be. But I wasn't like for sure about it.

Q: Did you know it was against the rules to use profanity with a teacher?
A: Yeah. Happens all the time. Most teachers are cool and understand, but that teacher is a bitch.

Q: Do you remember what were you thinking right before you decided to leave school?
A: I was thinking about how stupid school is, and how Xavier talks about all the things he does when he skips school.

Q: How did you feel after you left campus?

A: It was kind of exciting at first, but then I didn't know where to go or what to do.

Q: How did you find Xavier?

A: I went to the store across the street and sweet-talked the kid behind the counter into letting me use his phone. Xavier came and met me there.

Q: I see. Do you sometimes have trouble making plans in your head?

A: What do you mean?

Q: I mean do you struggle to get all the details straight? Like this plan to leave school or maybe even in class when your teacher assigns a paper or project?

A: Yeah. It gets all jumbled up, and I don't know what to do next, so I just sit there. Or I call Xavier. [laughs]

Q: What would happen if you got help before making a plan? Like asking for advice?

A: I don't know. Maybe I would do better in school.

Q: How would it make you feel to be more organized and better in school?

A: [shrugs] I guess that would be cool.

Parent Interview with Aisha

Q: When did Rochelle begin experiencing problems at school due to her behavior?

A: Her grades weren't slipping at all. Timothy told me she's been distracted in class, but other than that, I thought things were fine. Then, she started going with Xavier, and things started to change.

Q: Have you noticed Rochelle being distracted at home?

A: Yes. Sometimes she will get up during a TV show and go do something else. She will start chores and not finish them. Things like that.

Q: What are the circumstances surrounding Rochelle's distractibility?

A: I will tell her to do something, like set the table for dinner. She will get all the plates, silverware and cups out. Then, I'll go check, and they might all just be sitting on the table not set.

Q: How do you handle behavior problems at home?

A: DeMarcas and I try to redirect the kids. We try to talk a lot about why something is important to do or not do. Sometimes, I have to get stern. I'll use my "Mom" voice and say, "Now, Rochelle. Get up and go complete that right now." Generally, she does. If not, we take away privileges. Sometimes, honestly, I just let it go. Like the table. I'll just set it myself. Or Randall might come help me. Randall's not much of a problem at all, but sometimes I just don't have the energy to fight Rochelle.

Q: Are there any factors that could be causing stress in Rochelle's life?

A: Other than that idiot boyfriend? I knew that boy was trouble! She hasn't seen her birth mom since I don't know when. Birth mom keeps saying she wants to see the kids, then she screws up and can't. We've stopped telling them anything about her. They don't ask so we don't say anything.

Q: What are your thoughts as to what could be contributing to distractibility?

A: I followed up with our family doctor. He recommended an evaluation for ADHD. That could be it, but really it could be all this stuff happening with the boyfriend too. Or it could be some combination. I don't know. This whole situation is just exhausting.

Q: What else should be considered in addressing Rochelle's distractibility?

A: She can't lose focus on her education or music. She needs to finish school to get a good job, and the music is what she loves. She's going to need that passion to get her through the tough years to come. We have to get her refocused on what really matters. I've been praying about this. So has DeMarcas and his congregation. I believe she can get back on the right track.

Teacher Interview with Michelle

Q: Did you see any evidence that Rochelle has been distracted in your class?

A: Sometimes. She has a little trouble getting started in class.

Q: Are there other times she is distracted?

A: Sometimes, she gets distracted by the other students, especially if someone is clowning around or off-key. But overall, she does pretty well.

Q: What does it look like when Rochelle is distracted?

A: She turns around and looks toward whatever it is that is distracting her. Sometimes, though, I've noticed she just appears lost in thought. She will start picking at her fingernails or pulling at her jacket sleeves. She always wears a jacket. I didn't think it was that cool in my room, but I am up moving around a lot. She doesn't seem to bother the other students.

Q: Are there any settings or situations when the behavior does not occur?
A: If I am working with her or her section, she pays attention.

Q: Who is present when Rochelle is distracted?
A: The full class and me of course.

Q: What is happening prior to her distraction?
A: We are usually practicing. I might be working with a specific section or individual and the other students have to wait while I sort that out. There is a group of boys that tend to laugh and make comments under their breath. Quiet enough so I won't hear, but loud enough so that the students around them do. That has bothered Rochelle. But the boys don't do that all the time. Sometimes, I notice she's just staring at her hands or sleeves.

Q: What happens immediately following her behavior?
A: I call her name, and she snaps back to what we are doing.

Q: Are there any other behaviors that you notice occurring along with her distractibility?
A: No. Well, she does pick her fingernails badly. And I don't really understand the jacket. It's been fairly warm outside lately. But no behaviors to speak of.

Q: Can you think of a reason why Rochelle might be distracted?
A: I just assumed she had something on her mind.

Q: What would be a more acceptable way for Rochelle to stay on task?
A: She doesn't bother anyone. Like I said, I just say her name, and she snaps back.

Once Becky compiled the interview information, she asked Timothy to gather data on specific numbers of late assignments, tardies, and office referrals for sleeping in class. Timothy discovered Rochelle's teachers had written 10 discipline referrals for her sleeping in class. Timothy also noted a steady increase in the amount of tardies Rochelle was

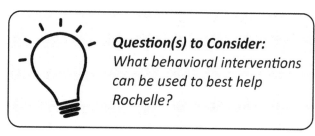

Question(s) to Consider:
What behavioral interventions can be used to best help Rochelle?

collecting. She was now at five tardies per week. The teachers also reported to Timothy that she no longer turned in work on time, or at all. Timothy gathered data on Rochelle's late and missing assignments.

Class	Late Assignments	Never Turned in Assignments
Table 5.3 • Frequency Chart for Rochelle's Behavior for the Last Nine Weeks		
Science	////////	////
History	/////	//
Math	/////////	///
Band	//	
Physical Education		
Language Arts/Reading	////	///

Your Task

You are now familiar with the parts of an FBA and a BIP. You also have behavior data from observations conducted by members of Rochelle's IEP team. Rochelle's behavior is becoming increasingly more disruptive, thus the IEP team needs to address the issues. Given the information regarding Rochelle's violations of the Student Code of Conduct and John's determination to use punitive discipline, there is an added layer of placement and LRE that must be discussed. Your task is as follows:

1. Assume the role of Becky, the behavior specialist. Complete an FBA as needed using the information provided in this chapter. Some forms will integrate this step into writing the BIP. Consult your state or district form for the exact procedure.

2. Develop a BIP based on the FBA you completed in Step 1.

Things to consider:

- Function of Rochelle's behavior
- Rochelle's violations of the Student Code of Conduct as manifestations of her disabling condition
- Educational placement considering LRE
- Behavioral support(s) to be successful

FBA/BIP Resources

Alberto, P. A., & Troutman, A. C. (2017). *Applied behavior analysis for teachers (9th edition)*. Upper Saddle River, NJ: Pearson.

General FBA/BIP Guidelines – www.behaviorbabe.com

High Leverage Practices – www.highleveragepractices.org/socialemotionalbehavioral

IRIS Center Modules – www.iris.peabody.vanderbilt.edu (click on Resources > IRS Resource Locator > Behavior and Classroom Management – at this point there are activities and case studies, and online modules that will take you through FBAs, BIPs, and data collection practice)

Figure 5.2. FBA/BIP Resources

References

Individuals with Disabilities Education Improvement Act, 20 U.S.C. § 1400 (2004).

The IRIS Center. (2009). *Functional behavioral assessment: Identifying the reasons for problem behavior and developing a behavior plan.* Retrieved from www.iris.peabody.vanderbilt.edu/module/fba

United States Department of Education (2012). Restraint and seclusion: Resource document. Retrieved from https://sites.ed.gov/idea/files/restraints-and-seclusion-resources.pdf

Wolf, T. L., McLaughlin, T. F., & Williams, R. L. (2006). Time-out interventions and strategies: A brief review and recommendations. *International Journal of Special Education, 21*(3), 22-29.

CHAPTER 6

Rochelle Plans for Graduation: Writing Transition Plans

This chapter concludes Rochelle's case study by discussing her needs for successful high school completion, including post-secondary education and community support. In this chapter, you will read about the required components of the Individualized Transition Plan (ITP) and explore Rochelle's need for the ITP as she prepares for graduation. As you consider ITPs, keep these questions in mind:

- What is the purpose of an ITP?
- When are ITPs to be addressed in the IEP?
- What is the purpose of teaching self-determination skills to students?

Discussion of Transition Plans

This section provides the reader with information relevant to the ITP that will help you complete the transition plan for Rochelle. Transition services is a term commonly used when referring to ITPs. The Individuals with Disabilities Education Improvement Act (2004) states that transition services need to be addressed by the time a student turns 16 years of age. Many states encourage the discussion of transition to begin at age 14, if not earlier.

Definition

Transition services are specified in the IDEIA (2004). Transition services are activities which are results-oriented and are based on the individual needs of the child with a disability (IDEIA, 2004). Because schools are required to plan for the future of a student with disabilities, it must be included in the Individualized Education Plan (IEP). The transition plan will include goals for the student after high school, and the steps necessary in reaching those goals.

Purpose

According to IDEIA (2004), transition services must begin at, or before, age 16. Transition plans are part of a student's IEP to ensure adequate skills for success after high school. Goals are written based on the interests of the student. Goals should focus on community participation, post-secondary education goals, independent living, and/or vocational skills. The IEP team will also determine which services, whether in school or out of school, the student needs to achieve their post high school goals.

Necessary Legal Components

There are several parts required by IDEIA in a student's transition plan. It is important that you review your state's Technical Assistance Guide for clarity about your state regulations. Below is a list and a brief description of the required components.

- **Postsecondary goals**
  - When working on postsecondary goals, remember that not all areas need to be addressed for each student. It depends upon the individual student.
  - To determine appropriate goals, the team must review the transition assessments(s) and identify strengths, interests, and needs.
  - It is recommended that postsecondary goals be measurable; however, consult your state guide for specific regulations.
  - Four areas can be addressed when writing postsecondary goals. You must write either a vocational goal or a post-secondary goal.
    - **Vocational Goals** should include the skills needed to perform a specific job.
      - *Example:* After high school, Bobbie will apprentice with a landscaping company and learn to use the equipment appropriately.
    - **Postsecondary Education Goals** focus on the skills needed to attend a college or university, a technical school, or even the military.
      - *Example:* After graduation, Dixie will attend the Universal Technical Institute.
    - **Job and Employment Goals** should focus on the skills needed to find, obtain, and keep a job.
      - *Example:* After high school, Dominique will work as a barista at the local coffee shop.
    - **Independent Living Goals** relate to the skills needed to live independently. These skills can include daily living, independent living, transportation, and personal finance.
      - *Example:* After graduation, Jorge will open a checking account.

○ When writing goals, you will need to incorporate transition services or activities. These services and/or activities are the steps needed to achieve the specific transition goal.

○ You will also need to include the person or the agency responsible for supporting the student in meeting the transition goal.

- **Transition Services**

○ Transition services are necessary for students with disabilities to meet their transition goals (Lee, n.d.). These transition services can be divided into five domains.

   ▪ **Instruction** - What type of instruction will be provided to the student? *For example*, will the student need instruction in paying bills or using the public transportation system?

   ▪ **Related services** - What related services, if any, are needed to assist the student in reaching their transition goals? *For example*, will the student need to coordinate special transportation or course release time for job training? These may be similar to what is already written in the IEP but should be addressed again in the transition plan.

   ▪ **Community experiences** – What interactions in real-world settings does the student need to master in order to be a functioning and satisfied member of the local community? *For example*, does the student need training in grocery shopping or attending public events?

   ▪ **Career and college counseling** – What information does the student need in order to access post-secondary education? This includes exploring, applying to, and attending post-secondary education. *For example*, does the

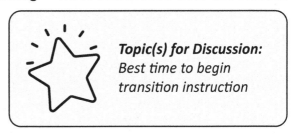

Topic(s) for Discussion:
Best time to begin transition instruction

student need assistance in completing a Free Application for Federal Student Aid (FAFSA) or information about attending a technical school instead of a traditional college?

   ▪ **Daily living skills** – What are the necessary tasks in which the student should participate for regular, everyday life routines? This can include shopping for groceries, cooking, laundry, washing and drying dishes.

- **Legal Considerations**

○ Transfer of Rights

- This occurs when the child reaches the age of majority under state law, usually age 18.

- When the transfer of rights occurs, the legal decision becomes the responsibility of the student, unless the student is deemed unable to make decisions for themselves due to cognitive impairments or other similar impairments.

- The student and families must be informed of these rights a year before they reach age of majority and should be documented in the IEP.

- All rights transfer unless the parents will continue to have legal guardianship after the child reaches the age of majority.

Self-Determination

When discussing transition plans, it is highly recommended that educators begin, if not continue, teaching self-determination skills. According to the National Parent Center on Transition and Employment (n.d.), self-determination is the attitudes and beliefs of an individual to set goals for themselves. It is important that educators teach self-determination skills to *all* students, but even more so to older students. Self-determination skills allow students with disabilities to advocate for themselves by teaching them how to solve problems, take control and responsibility for themselves, and make their own choices (National Parent Center on Transition and Employment, n.d.). One-way educators can assist students with self-determination skills is to have the student attend and possibly run their IEP meeting.

Everyone has the right to dream about their future, and we are all guaranteed the right to pursue happiness in this country. Students with disabilities should be no exception. There are many famous individuals with disabilities who overcame stifling obstacles to accomplish great things, and our society is becoming more supportive of individuals with disabilities all the time. However, how do we support the hopes and dreams

Question(s) to Consider:
How do you balance the needs of the students with their personal aspirations and dreams?

of students with disabilities when their dreams seem out of reach or when their hopes are well beyond their documented skills? This is the paradox the transition professional faces during this process: the balance of support with the realistic wisdom of life.

Case Study

As you read the case study, consider the following key questions:

- What support does Rochelle need for independent living?
- What post-secondary training or education does Rochelle need?
- How can the stakeholders support Rochelle's self-determined goals?

Rochelle's transition to high school was uneventful after a very smooth exit from middle school. Her middle school teachers monitored Rochelle closely, and not wanting to be removed from her current foster home, Rochelle responded positively. She focused on passing her classes and her music. As a result, at the end of eighth grade, Rochelle was playing all the woodwinds, but is showing a distinct talent for the clarinet as well as the saxophone. She now plays in the school band, in church, and at community events.

In high school, Rochelle follows the standard graduation pathway. She is assigned to Grace's case load. Grace supervises one-third of the students with disabilities (based on the beginning letter of their last name) along with the other special education teachers. Grace plays the guitar, so a strong rapport with Rochelle was almost immediate.

As a freshman, Rochelle stated that she wanted to be a professional musician. Grace helped her complete several career inventories, personality tests, and job searches. Rochelle still insisted on becoming a professional musician despite her inventory results indicating that she was well-suited for a career in audio-visual technical skills, such as a motion picture projectionist or an equipment technician. Grace talked with Aisha, and they decided to support Rochelle's career goal to pursue becoming a musician.

Gordon has been the high school band director for 15 years. His band consistently won national awards. Many community members attend the high school football games not as much to support the team, but to see the halftime show. Gordon's band has 150 members and regularly features small ensembles. Many of Gordon's former students received significant college music scholarships. He is proud of his program and what they accomplish. He has very high standards, and he is very selective about who participates.

Michelle, Rochelle's middle school band teacher, approached Gordon after a middle school band concert. Gordon always attends the Spring Concert to scout for his future freshmen. Rochelle was featured, and Gordon was initially very excited to get her started in his program. He was less excited, however, when he asked Michelle about her. When she stated that Rochelle "has been through a lot" Gordon was suspicious. Michelle then went on to describe how much music helped Rochelle with her "learning and attention challenges" and that she was certain the high school band "will help Rochelle stay on the right track." Gordon dismissed

Rochelle immediately after hearing this. He did not have the time or patience to worry about some freshman causing trouble in his program. He initially refused to allow Rochelle to be enrolled in his band class, telling the high school counselor to place her in a general music class instead. It was Grace who explained that Rochelle would be an asset and that she deserved a chance. After a lengthy, tense conversation, Gordon agreed that Rochelle could attend Summer Band Camp. He would make his final decision then.

Grace worked with DeMarcas and the mentorship program closely. She explained that Summer Band Camp was basically Rochelle's audition for band. DeMarcas clearly outlined to Rochelle what she needed to do, and Rochelle did everything she was instructed. She was highly motivated to join the band. Her talent and discipline impressed Gordon, and he permitted her to join band. It was not long before Rochelle was outperforming upperclassmen. However, Gordon was constantly having to watch Rochelle's grades, and he arranged for some of the other band students to tutor her. He really believed he would lose Rochelle when she was required to take Spanish, and she was barely passing her math and English classes. Ultimately, with a few close scares, Rochelle made it.

Thanks to Gordon, Rochelle was offered the opportunity to be a volunteer at the community music hall as part of the city's "Young Ambassadors" program. On opening night during the Performing Arts series, Rochelle and 14 other high school-aged volunteers spent the evening showing guests to their seats, running errands for staff, or helping the talent backstage. Rochelle loved it. She was one of only two Young Ambassadors who were offered a part-time job once the season ended. Rochelle spent as much time as she could at the community music hall doing any job she was asked. Some of the local symphony performers would play "jam" sessions with her after rehearsals. She made many friends and even met some famous performers.

During the Performing Arts series of her senior year, Rochelle was working backstage when a well-known singer performed. The singer had attended the same high school as Rochelle. The two immediately became friends, and the singer stayed in touch with Rochelle through social media. Aisha was skeptical at first, but as she also was included in the communication, she learned that the singer was a warm, generous person. She had a tough upbringing too, so she related to Rochelle's struggles. The singer encouraged Rochelle to finish high school strong, and Rochelle responded positively to the motivation. At one point, the singer informed Rochelle that she had been offered a 6-month contract by a casino in Las Vegas. She mentioned that Rochelle might want a job as her junior assistant the summer after she graduated from high school. If she was interested, she encouraged Rochelle to apply through her business manager. Rochelle was ecstatic! About the same time, Aisha and Grace met with Rochelle to finalize her plans for the future and discuss her transfer of rights.

Randall, Rochelle's brother, graduated from high school two years before. He decided to join the U.S. Navy, and so he was gone. Rochelle missed him deeply. Even though Aisha and DeMarcas were never able to adopt Randall and Rochelle, they were a family. Now, it was Rochelle's turn to graduate from high school. Believing her summer job secure, Rochelle could not wait to finish high school and move to Las Vegas.

Stakeholder Perspectives

Transition is a time when stakeholders are vital. Each stakeholder's unique perspective on the student is important to adequately plan for a smooth transition into the adult system. Often, frank discussions about possible challenges or barriers are necessary to help the individual with disabilities prepare for the world. However, these discussions need to be tempered with support for the individual's personal aspirations, hopes, and dreams.

Topic(s) for Discussion: Transfer of Rights; Student-Led IEP meetings; Coordinating services for (a) Department of Family and Protective Services, (b) Department of Assistive and Rehabilitation Services, and (c) Vocational Rehabilitation

While realism is important, every individual, whether disabled or not, has the right to fight for the future they want.

Foster Parent Concerns

Initially, Aisha and DeMarcas were skeptical of Rochelle's friendship with the famous singer. While they relaxed their concerns, they still worried about Rochelle's decision to move to Las Vegas as an 18-year-old. The situation seemed too good to be true, but not wanting to deny Rochelle any opportunity, they reluctantly supported her. The cost of traveling and moving to Las Vegas was discussed, and Rochelle planned to use the money she saved from her part-time job and community performances to cover those costs. Aisha and DeMarcas could think of no more objections. They helped her plan the move.

General Education Teacher Concerns

Gordon could not believe how talented Rochelle had become. Nor could he believe that she had a potential opportunity to work for a famous singer in such a venue. He expressed concern to Grace that Rochelle's lack of academic skill, which he referred to as "smarts," might impede her success. Can she manage money if she can't pass math without a tutor? Can she read and sign a lease if she can't pass English without help? Who's going to watch her to make sure she doesn't slip up or make a bad decision? While Gordon wanted Rochelle to be successful, he highly doubted that she could make it on her own.

Special Education Teacher Concerns

Grace wants all these opportunities to work out for Rochelle. Knowing her background, Grace wants Rochelle to be the poster child for good things happening in life. Grace worked hard to cram in lessons about budgeting, how to rent an apartment, how to vet a roommate, and how to book a flight so Rochelle can come home for the holidays. While Rochelle is not always attentive, Grace knows some of the information will get through. She is also trying to be Rochelle's greatest cheerleader with the other stakeholders involved.

Vocational Rehabilitation Specialist Concerns

Grace always includes the local vocational rehabilitation specialists in her transition IEP meetings. This year, DeWayne is covering her regional area. DeWayne has been a Vocational Rehabilitation Counselor for 12 years. Grace was disappointed that DeWayne was moved to her area. From conversations with colleagues who had worked with him in the past, she learned that DeWayne was not proactive in helping students, and he often missed IEP meetings. Grace emailed him for his input before the meeting, and DeWayne responded that he was not sure he could attend. He provided his contact information to share with Rochelle and her family.

Administrator Concerns

Khem is a former biology teacher and basketball coach who received his principal licensure through alternative certification programming. When a position opened at the high school for an assistant principal, he was thrilled to be selected. He cares about all his "kids" and wants them to succeed. However, IEP meetings are not his highest priority. He usually comes in just as the meeting begins, shakes hands with the parent(s) and student, signs what he needs to, and leaves as quickly as possible. He is aware of Rochelle mostly because Randall was in his class and played basketball on his team. He defers to the special education team as the experts and supports their recommendations.

Social Worker Concerns

Amanda, quite frankly, is exhausted. She has been with Rochelle for years now, and it is coming to an end. Amanda had to fight often to keep Randall and Rochelle on her case load. She fought against transfers, reorganizations, and new administrative policies. Finally, she watched Randall graduate and leave for the military, and now Rochelle is graduating with the potential of a fabulous career ahead of her. Amanda is eligible to retire, so she wants this last case to close positively. She simply wants a solid transition plan to ensure graduation and for Rochelle to get on with her adult life.

Assessment Results

Grace compiled the transition evaluation data and reports the following information to the IEP team:

Rochelle is a determined and talented teen who reported that she enjoys music and streaming new television shows. She participates in high school band and is regularly featured as a soloist. She currently works as a "Young Ambassador" at the community music hall. In her interview, Rochelle reported that she wants a job in the music industry. Specifically, she wants to play in a famous band or for a famous singer. She currently has no plans to attend higher education or any postsecondary training program. While all the adults involved in Rochelle's life have expressed concern about her plan to move to Las Vegas, Rochelle is determined that

Question(s) to Consider:
Rochelle is only concerned about the job opportunity in Las Vegas. What else should she be considering? How do you guide her into thinking about these things?

this is her path. As such, she acknowledges that she needs help with money management and finding a place to live. She also expressed concern over learning how to use the Las Vegas bus system.

Recent evaluation results from the current IEP indicate that Rochelle still qualifies as having Other Health Impairments (OHI) for Attention Deficit/Hyperactivity Disorder, Combined Type and a mild-moderate impairment in attention and executive functioning (based in part on her IQ of 70) qualifying her as Learning Disabled (LD). All testing is current. Rochelle has difficulty focusing in class, especially in areas she struggles in, like math and language arts. Rochelle does not drive due to the ease of using the city bus system and a lack of interest in taking another class.

Independent Living

Although Rochelle's foster parents express concern over her ability to manage money well or handle an apartment lease, Rochelle has many independent living skills. Her assessment results indicate she is capable of activities of daily living including grooming, cleaning, time management, and cooking. Rochelle reports feeling inadequate with managing money, especially when it comes to budgeting and shopping. She reports understanding how to take care of herself, including eating well-balanced meals, attending to her personal health needs (e.g., managing her menstrual cycles), and seeking medical help when she is sick. Since she is exiting the foster care system when she completes high school and turns 18, Rochelle knows she must live independently, and she is excited to have "her own space."

Post-Secondary Education

Rochelle's personality inventories indicate that she is an introvert who loves music and nature and shows a preference for kinesthetic learning. She would be best suited in a supportive job where she can work under direction but with independence. Her career inventories indicate that she is best suited for the following jobs: (a) musician, instrumental, (b) musical instrument repairer and tuner, (c) broadcast technician, and (d) secretary or administrative assistant, except legal, medical and executive. Rochelle has no plans to attend higher education or postsecondary training. She is focused on moving to Las Vegas to accept a position, that she has not yet been offered, with a singer she met while working at the community music hall. She says she is done with school.

Community Support

Rochelle will likely need resources to help her find an apartment, set up a bank account, manage her money, and use public transportation. She may also need strategies to connect to groups and activities in her new community that align with her interests. For example, she may need to know how to join a gym, find a faith community where she can continue to participate in a music ministry, or join a local group of musicians that perform at charitable events.

Your Task

The process of assisting a student who is transitioning to adulthood is complicated. You must examine each aspect of life (e.g., independent living, education, career development) without overwhelming the student in the process. You need to know about community resources (i.e., coordinating with the Department of Family and Protective Services for students who were in foster care, Department of Assistive and Rehabilitative Services for students with disabling conditions, and support services on local post-secondary campuses such as Disability Services and TRIO). It is also vital that you consider your student's hopes and dreams. In Rochelle's case, she has big dreams that may or may not match her skill level.

Your task is as follows:

1. Determine Rochelle's future goals and how you will address those in the ITP.

2. Assume the role of Grace when writing the ITP. Using your state's transition form, develop an appropriate ITP for Rochelle. You need to complete *all* relevant sections of the ITP.

Things to consider:

- Community resources
- Supporting services in Las Vegas
- Services Rochelle needs as she begins her new job
- Trainings and/or information needed to prepare for her upcoming transition

---

Transition Resources

IRIS Center Modules – www.iris.peabody.vanderbilt.edu (click on Resources > IRS Resource Locator > Transition > Modules)

National Technical Assistance Center on Transition – www.transitionta.org /transitionplanning

PACER Center – www.pacer.org/students/transition-to-life

Sample IEP Forms – www.understood.org (find the search bar and type in "Download: Sample IEP Transition Plan and Goals")

The Center for Parent Information and Resources – www.parentcenter hub.org/iep-transition

Figure 6.1. Transition Resources

References

Individuals with Disabilities Education Improvement Act, 20 U.S.C. § 300.43 (2004).

Lee, A. L. (n.d.). IEP Transition Planning: Preparing for Young Adulthood. Retrieved from www.understood.org/en/school-learning/special-services/ieps/iep-transition-planning-preparing-for-young-adulthood

Conclusion

The complex process of writing the necessary special education documents to ensure services are delivered appropriately can be daunting. Very few students will have simple, straightforward diagnoses, and many have complicated home lives too. With the number of stakeholders involved, and the corresponding number of superfluous opinions provided, the entire process can become overwhelming and stressful. However, the informed special education professional can separate opinion from evidence-based fact and write the documents that truly support the success of the individual with special needs.

This guide was arranged chronologically, utilizing the relevant special education documents as Rochelle entered, progressed in, and exited the educational system. In Chapter 1, you learned how to use this book. In Chapter 2, you were provided some general guiding principles for technical writing. In Chapter 3, you reviewed writing documents for young children with disabilities and worked towards

Topic(s) for Discussion:
Current outcomes for individuals with disabilities - the good, the bad, and the ugly

creating an IFSP. In Chapter 4, you worked through the keystone document in special education, the IEP. In Chapter 5, you examined data to add a behavior plan and the components of the FBA. Finally, in Chapter 6, you concluded Rochelle's journey by developing a transition plan to exit school and enter adulthood.

You have followed the special education journey of Rochelle. While Rochelle is fictional, the circumstances of her case are based upon actual experiences and situations the authors faced. Drawing upon collective experience, the goal was to help you prepare for the complexities that you will face as a special educator. Not only did you see Rochelle struggle, but you saw the stakeholders struggle as well. If you ever experience difficulty determining the next best step for your student with disabilities,

Question(s) to Consider:
How do you stay motivated to help your students when you are discouraged by what you see?

you are not alone. If you face a stakeholder whose opinions vary widely from yours about what the correct plan should be, you are not alone. If you struggle with how the educational system determines services are to be delivered, you are certainly not alone. There are many of us who have experienced the same things, and there are many resources available to help you find the answers. Rely on your larger special education community. Most of us are happy to help each other along the path. You are not in it alone!

For those of you just beginning your career serving individuals with special needs, here is a personal word of encouragement from each of the authors:

Dr. Andrea Hathcote: I have worked in numerous positions in schools and with a wide variety of disabling conditions, from mild to profound. I am also the parent of a child with special needs, so I sat on each side of the IEP table; as a professional and as a parent. I can tell you that I was much more comfortable as a professional. No matter how much you think you know walking into the IEP meeting, when someone, even someone you respect, begins to tell you all the things your child cannot do, your parental brain immediately shifts into defense mode. Looking back, I am troubled by the lack of sympathy I displayed to parents early in my career. After becoming a parent of a child with special needs, both my professionalism and empathy increased. If you are not a parent, that is no condemnation of your ability to be an utterly amazing educator! We need your objective point of view and your focus on results. Just remember to be patient with the parents who are struggling with the reality of their child's weaknesses. Maintain your professionalism tempered with friendliness and respect. If you, like me, must straddle the line between professional and parent, remember your role in the meeting. Do not try to run the meeting as a parent, and do not lose your focus as a professional. Overall, I believe that all students know when they are cared for and supported. I also believe that all students (and parents) can tell insincerity and underlying animosity or judgment. Like healthcare professionals, we educators must have well-developed clinical and bedside manners. We must write and meet the goals while providing the appropriate level of caring and support. It is a fine line that quite frankly I often had trouble managing. Remember that self-care goes a long way. Your students do not care what happened in your life last night or this morning. They care about how you are treating them today, right now. Take care of yourself emotionally and physically so that when you enter the classroom you are ready to serve the most vulnerable population in our educational system today. We are counting on you! I believe in you! Thank you for choosing this career!

Dr. Kathleen Boothe: I have worked as a classroom teacher and in higher education where I prepare future special educators. I have been in your shoes and know that writing special education documents is not an easy task. It will become easier with time and practice. As a teacher you can only do so much, but you still must be prepared. You must always do what is in the best interest of the student. I tell my teacher education candidates, "Whether you are right or wrong, you must be able to defend what you are doing." This is so important because there are many aspects of special education that we may be unaware of, but ultimately the responsibility falls on you. Teaching in both public schools and higher education I have also discovered the importance of building relationships with your students and their families; this helps to build trust. Trust is imperative for you when it comes to educating students with disabilities. Finally, I learned the value and importance of belonging to a professional organization such as the Council for Exceptional Children (CEC). The colleagues I have met there inspire me, encourage me, and many have become my friends. Conferences are like family reunions, except with experts in special education who can help you become better at your job. I love that I can text, call, or email someone and receive clarification for anything I am unsure of or do not know. I highly encourage you to find a way to join a professional organization and become part of the larger community. Our collective voice can be heard, and we can make a difference for each other and our students.

Appendix A
Assessment Summary*

This appendix provides the reader with a summary of Rochelle's assessments. The assessment summary provided below, follows the formatting of a Special Education Comprehensive Report, found in the textbook *Assessment in Special Education: A Practical Approach* (Pierangelo & Giuliani, 2017). While this assessment summary is not as in depth as a comprehensive assessment report, we wanted to provide the reader with the relevant information for writing an IEP, all in one easy to read area. The reader will still need to interpret the information and draw their own conclusions based on their interpretation.

Sample Public Schools Sample, State Privileged and Confidential Information	
Name of Student: Rochelle Student	**School:** Sample Elementary
Address: 1 Main Street, Sample, ST, 88899	**Teacher:** Mirah Teacher
Phone #: 903-333-1234	**Referred By:** Jaime Principal
Date of Birth: 09/05/2011	**Date of Testing:** 11/11/2020
Grade: 4	**Date of Report:** 11/16/2020
Chronological Age: 9 years, 2 months	**Examiner:** Delores Psychologist
Parents Names: Aisha and DeMarcas Parent	

Reason for Referral

Rochelle Student was referred for an evaluation of a suspected learning disability. This evaluation is intended to answer the following questions: What cognitive, language, and/or academic strengths and weaknesses exist? What are Rochelle's cognitive, language, and academic developmental levels?

Background History

Below is a brief summary of Rochelle's background history, for more detailed background information, refer to Chapters 3 and 4.

Family History: Rochelle Student lives at home with her foster mother and father, Aisha and DeMarcas Parent, and biological brother, Randall. Her foster mother works as a church secretary, and her foster father works full-time as a minister. The foster parents have lived in Sample for many years, and Rochelle and Randall joined their family from a previous foster placement.

Developmental History: A record review shows that Rochelle was born at a local hospital and there were no complications. From birth to age three, there is no data indicating Rochelle's development. She and her brother were separated from their biological parents when Rochelle was three due to abuse and extreme neglect. When entering the first foster placement, Rochelle was developmentally, physically, emotionally, and educationally delayed. She was able to make rapid progress both at her home and through Head Start.

Rochelle speaks English at home and best expressed herself orally. Her receptive English is average compared to her peers, and her expressive English is slightly below average compared to her peers. The student is not limited English proficient.

Rochelle's vision is within normal limits without glasses. Her hearing is also within normal limits without aids. Rochelle's health history does not indicate any significant issues. She does not appear to have any physical conditions which directly affect her ability to profit from the educational process. Therefore, adapted physical education is not indicated.

Rochelle lives with her foster parents. She loves music, watching television, and playing at the church. While she is overcoming her legacy of early abuse, Rochelle shows no concerns regarding cultural, linguistic, or experiential factors that influence her learning and behavioral patterns. She participated in Head Start and made good academic progress through third grade so there is no lack of previous educational opportunities in reading and/or math.

Academic History: Rochelle began Head Start at age three. Her teacher had concerns about her lack of speech and non-compliant behaviors in addition to her developmental delays. An Individualized Family Service Plan (IFSP) was put into place.

Before beginning Kindergarten, Rochelle and her brother were moved to their current foster placement. She had developed a vocabulary of 190 words, and she weighed 37 pounds and was 35 inches tall when she entered Kindergarten.

Although she was still very small compared to her peers, Rochelle ran and played just like they did. In elementary school, Rochelle made progress and caught up to her peers. She even met standards on her first standardized assessment in third grade.

In fourth grade, Mirah Teacher administered the DIBELS for reading and AIMSweb for Math within the first week of school.

DIBELS

Test	Score	Score Level
Composite Score	289	Below Benchmark
DORF Words Correct	80	Below Benchmark
DORF Accuracy	94	Below Benchmark
Retell Fluency	20	Below Benchmark

Score Goal Interpretation for beginning of school year

DIBELS Composite Score

0-244 = Well Below Benchmark

245-289 = Below Benchmark

290-886 = At or Above Benchmark

DORF Words Correct

0-69 = Well Below Benchmark

70-89 = Below Benchmark

90-350 = At or Above Benchmark

DORF Accuracy

0-92 = Well Below Benchmark

93-95 = Below Benchmark

96-100 = At or Above Benchmark

Retell Fluency

27-94 = Well Below Benchmark

14-25 = Below Benchmark

27-94 = At or Above Benchmark

AIMSweb for Math

Subtest	Score	Percentile	Level
Computation and Application	4	Below 15%	Below Average
Computation	10	Below 15%	Below Average

Scale of performance levels for AIMSweb for Math are:
11th-25th Percentile = Below Average
26th-74th Percentile = Average
75th-89th Percentile = Above Average
90th-99th Percentile = Well-Above Average

Rochelle's scores were below average. As a result, Rochelle qualified for several Tier 2 level intervention programs, including Reading Recovery and enVisionMATH. Participation in these programs has not improved her progress. Mirah is very worried about Rochelle's lack of academic skills. Her assessment results demonstrate that Rochelle is well behind in alphabetic principle, fluency, and number recognition. The only subjects in which Rochelle exhibits any type of interest or skill is in music, art, and physical education.

Rochelle was also administered the KeyMath 3 at age 9 years and 2 months, which generated the following results:

KeyMath 3

Composite Test	Scaled Score	Grade Equivalent	Percentile	Level
Basic Concepts	72	1.7	3%	Below Average
Subtest	Scaled Score	Grade Equivalent	Notes (use this for your own personal notes)	
Numeration	4	1.4		
Algebra	5	1.8		
Geometry	7	2.2		
Measurement	7	2.4		
Data Analysis & Probability	3	K.5		

(continued on next page)

(KeyMath 3 continued)

Composite Test	Scaled Score	Grade Equivalent	Percentile	Level
Operations	84	3.1	14%	Below Average
Subtest	Scaled Score	Grade Equivalent	Notes (use this for your own personal notes)	
Mental Computation & Estimation	5	2.1		
Addition & Subtraction	8	3.5		
Multiplication & Division	10	4.2		
Composite Test	Scaled Score	Grade Equivalent	Percentile	Level
Applications	73	1.8	4%	Below Average
Subtest	Scaled Score	Grade Equivalent	Notes (use this for your own personal notes)	
Foundations of Problem Solving	5	1.8		
Applied Problem Solving	5	1.5		
Composite Test	Scaled Score	Grade Equivalent	Percentile	Level
Total Test	72	2.2	5%	Below Average

Standard scores for the KeyMath 3 are:

Below 70 = Well-Below Average

70-85 = Below Average

85-115 = Average

115-130 = Above Average

Above 130 = Well-Above Average

Below is an copy of Rochelle's most recent report card grades.

Subject	Grade
Reading	82
Math	64
Language Arts	80
Science	88
Social Studies	83
Art	Exemplary
Health	Exemplary
PE	100
Music	100
Computer	100

Social History: According to Rochelle's foster parents, Rochelle struggled with the transition to the new home. Aisha offered to teach Rochelle to play the piano, and those lessons seemed to help Rochelle with the transition. Rochelle is very social, sometimes too social, and needs lots of redirection regarding social boundaries. She will tantrum when she does not get her way, but she is trying hard to do well in school.

Parent's Perception of the Problems: Behavioral observations from the foster parents indicate that Rochelle has emotional outbursts at home. She will cry, shout, pout, and withdraw from an activity or group when she is upset, but eventually accepts the limitations placed on her. She does change her eating habits if she is upset. When not in school, Rochelle enjoys music, playing at the church, and interacting with the family.

Aisha told the principal that she cannot come to the school three days a week to pick Rochelle up when she tantrums. DeMarcas tried to help with Rochelle, but she refuses to talk to him when she is upset. She only wants Aisha. As a result, the bulk of Rochelle's care falls on Aisha. Rochelle does not tantrum much at home, but Aisha reports being very tired at the end of the day because Rochelle is so needy. Although she is finally eating some, Rochelle has lost weight again, and Aisha is concerned.

Behavioral Observations

Classroom Observations

Behavioral observations from the classroom teacher indicate that Rochelle will pout and withdraw from the activity or group when she is upset. She also appears to have a short attention span for reading and math. It is difficult to keep her on task in large and small groups. The classroom teacher was asked to compare Rochelle to her peers. The teacher reported Rochelle was average in the areas of (a) generally cooperates or is compliant with teacher request, (b) adapts to new situations without getting upset, (c) makes and keep friends at school, (d) works cooperatively with others, (e) has an even and happy disposition, (f) is pleased with good work, (g) initiates activities independently, and (h) responds appropriately to praise and correction. The teacher reports Rochelle is below average in accepting responsibility for her own actions. Finally, the teacher reports Rochelle is poor in resisting becoming discouraged by difficulties and minor setbacks. While the teacher raises some behavioral concerns, Rochelle's behavior both in school and out of school does not appear to influence learning and education placement, programming, or discipline.

Initial Interview with Student

Rochelle was brought to the examiner's office before testing for an initial interview. Rochelle appeared anxious and kept asking if she was in trouble. The examiner explained that she was not in trouble at all; she was there to do a little work to see if she needed any extra help in class. Rochelle appeared to calm down then. The examiner asked what Rochelle liked best about school. Rochelle responded that she liked PE, art, and computer. She expressed that she really liked music the best. Rochelle said she did not like reading much, and she stated that she hated math. She also said she did not like her teacher (Mirah) because she did not help her right. Rochelle said she did not like looking stupid to her friends. When the examiner thanked Rochelle for sharing all that information and told her it was time to start the work, Rochelle sighed and asked if she had to. When the examiner responded affirmatively, Rochelle sighed again but agreed to participate.

Behavior During Testing

Rochelle was cooperative throughout the testing process. She appeared at ease, comfortable, and attentive. She did appear to tire slightly, but persisted throughout the process. She responded slowly and carefully to test questions and persisted even when tasks became more difficult. Therefore, the test results are considered valid and reliable.

Tests and Procedures Administered

- Woodcock-Johnson III Tests of Cognitive Abilities (WJ-III)
- Wechsler Intelligence Scale for Children IV (WISC-IV)
- Wechsler Individual Achievement Test Second Edition (WIAT-III)
- Vineland Adaptive Behavior Scales

Test Results

Use the tables below as an opportunity to interpret Rochelle's test scores and determine her IEP goals.

Rochelle was administered the Woodcock-Johnson III Tests of Cognitive Abilities at age 9 years and 2 months, which generated the following results:

Subtest	Composite Score	Percentile	Grade Equivalent	Level
GIA (EXT)	89	22%	2.6	Average/ Within Normal Limits
*Verbal Ability	104	60%	4.7	Average/ Within Normal Limits
**Thinking Ability	89	23%	2.4	Average/ Within Normal Limits
***Cognitive Efficiency	86	18%	2.8	Average/ Within Normal Limits
Comprehension - Knowledge	104	60%	4.7	Average/ Within Normal Limits
Long Term Retrieval	72	3%	1.4	Below Average/ Normative Weakness
Visual-Spatial Thinking	98	44%	3.7	Average/ Within Normal Limits
Auditory Processing	105	64%	6.1	Average/ Within Normal Limits
****Fluid Reasoning	80	9%	1.8	Below Average/ Normative Weakness
Processing Speed	95	38%	3.8	Average/ Within Normal Limits
Short-Term Memory	82	11%	1.7	Below Average/ Normative Weakness

(continued on next page)

(WJ-III continued)

Standardized results for the WJ-III are:

116-130 = Above Average/Normative Strength

85-115 = Average/Within Normal Limits

70-84 = Below Average/Normative Weakness

69 or below = Lower Extreme/Normative Weakness

*Verbal ability refers to breadth and depth of acquired knowledge, ability to communicate knowledge, ability to reason based on previous learning.

**Thinking ability refers to the ability to perceive, analyze, synthesize, think with visual patterns, ability to store and recall visual representations, and discriminate auditory information.

***Cognitive Efficiency refers to short-term memory and processing speed.

****Fluid Reasoning refers to mental operations used in a novel task that cannot be performed automatically.

Rochelle was administered the Wechsler Intelligence Scale for Children IV and the Wechsler Individual Achievement Test Third Edition at age 9 years and 2 months, which generated the following results:

Subtest	Composite Score	Percentile	Grade Equivalent	Level
Word Reading	102	55%	4.7	Average
Reading Comprehension	91	27%	2.8	Average
Pseudoword Decoding	110	75%	6.0	High Average
Numerical Operations	101	53%	4.4	Average
Math Reasoning	76	5%	2.2	Borderline
Written Expression	95	37%	3.2	Average
Matrix Reasoning = 70				Borderline/ Below Average

(continued on next page)

(WISC-IV and WIAT-III continued)

*Matrix Reasoning (based on results from WISC-IV) refers to the ability to use logic and solve a problem.

Standardized results for the WISC-IV are:

146-159 = Highly Gifted
130-145 = Moderately Gifted
120-129 = Above Average
110-119 = High Average
90-109 = Average
80-89 = Low Average
70-79 = Borderline/Below Average

Standard scores for the WIAT-III are:

Below 70 = Extremely Low
70-79 = Borderline
80-89 = Low Average
90-109 = Average
110-119 = High Average
120-129 = Superior
Above 130 = Very Superior

Rochelle was administered the Vineland Adaptive Behavior Scales at age 9 years and 2 months, which resulted in the following results:

Domain	Standard Score	Adaptive Level
Daily Living Skills	95	Adequate
Socialization	109	Adequate
Adaptive Behavior Composite	105	Adequate

Standardized results for the Vineland Adaptive Behavior Scales are:

130-140 = High Adaptive Level
115-129 = Moderately High Adaptive Level
86-114 = Adequate Adaptive Level
71-85 = Moderately Low Adaptive Level
20-70 = Low Adaptive Level

Rochelle's teacher was asked to compare Rochelle (age 9 years and 2 months) to her peers, which generated the following results:

- Generally cooperates or is compliant with teacher request: **Average**
- Adapts to new situations without getting upset: **Average**
- Accepts responsibility for own actions: **Below Average**
- Makes and keep friends at school: **Average**
- Works cooperatively with others: **Average**
- Has an even and happy disposition: **Average**
- Is pleased with good work: **Average**
- Initiates activities independently: **Average**
- Responds appropriately to praise and correction: **Average**
- Resists becoming discouraged by difficulties and minor setbacks: **Poor**

Conclusions

Rochelle Student is a 9-year-old student in fourth grade who was administered the above- referenced assessments. A wide range of areas were assessed, resulting in a wide range of scores from advanced to very limited.

The following is a list of Rochelle's greatest strengths and weaknesses. Her general areas of strength include: (a) verbal ability, (b) auditory processing, (c) verbal-knowledge (WJ-III). She demonstrates weakness in the areas of (a) long-term retrieval, (b) fluid reasoning, (c) short-term memory (WJ-III). Her standard IQ score was 70 (WISC-IV). She demonstrated adequate adaptive behavior (Vineland Adaptive Behavior Scales), but her teacher reported behavioral weaknesses where Rochelle: (a) accepts responsibility for own actions, and (b) resists becoming discouraged by difficulties and minor setbacks. In math, Rochelle demonstrates below average skills in all domains: (a) basic concepts, (b) operations, and (c) applications (KeyMath 3). In language arts, she demonstrated strength in pseudoword decoding and weakness in math reasoning (DIBELS). Classroom functioning in math shows that Rochelle is below the 15th percentile (AIMSweb for Math), and she is passing all classes except math (Report Card).

While the teacher raises some behavioral concerns, Rochelle's behavior both in school and out of school does not appear to influence learning and education placement, programming, or discipline. Results of testing, observation, history, and interviews all seem to indicate that Rochelle's pattern is similar to children with mild-moderate cognitive disabilities.

Recommendations

This section has been omitted so that the user can create their own goals and objectives when completing the IEP.

Written by: Delores Psychologist
School Psychologist

*This assessment summary is modeled after the comprehensive report found in Pierangelo, R. A., & Giuliani, G. (2017). *Assessment in Special Education: A Practical Approach* (5th ed.). Boston: Pearson.